The Shared Well

The Shared Well

A Concise Guide to Relations between Islam and the West

ROBERT VAN DE WEYER

Brassey's, Inc.

WASHINGTON, D.C.

John Hunt Publishing Ltd.
46a West Street
New Arlesford
Hants SO24 9AU
UK

Library of Congress Cataloging-in-Publication Data
Van de Weyer, Robert.
  The shared well : a concise guide to relations between Islam
and the West / Robert Van de Weyer. — 1st ed.
      p. cm.
Includes bibliographical references and index.
  ISBN 1-57488-564-2 (alk. paper)
  1. Religion and politics. 2. East and West. 3. Islam —
Relations — Christianity. 4. Christianity — Relations — Islam.
5. September 11 Terrorist Attacks, 2001. I. Title.
  BL65.P7 V36 2002
  303.48'2176710821 — dc21   2002003954

Printed in the United States of America on acid-free paper
that meets the American National Standards Institute Z39-48
Standard.

Brassey's, Inc.
22841 Quicksilver Drive
Dulles, Virginia 20166

Text design by Pen & Palette Unlimited

First Edition

10 9 8 7 6 5 4 3 2 1

Contents

Preface   vii

Introduction: Anguished Questions   1

Chapter 1   "Why do they hate us?"
Islam and the West in conflict   7
The Arab Empire ❂ *The Crusades* ❂
The Ottoman Empire ❂ *Western
Imperialism* ❂ *Islamic Militancy* ❂
Zionism ❂ *The Legacy*

Chapter 2   "Is mutual love and respect possible?"
Islam and the West in harmony   33
Christian Roots of Islam ❂ *Philosophy
and Theology* ❂ *Science, Mathematics,
and Medicine* ❂ *Politics and Law* ❂
Warfare ❂ *The Legacy*

Chapter 3   "What can we do—politically?"
The politics of peace   55
The Globalization of Goods and Capital ❂
False Assumptions ❂ *The Globalization
of People and Expertise* ❂ *Politics after
September 11* ❂ *Toward Political Freedom*

Chapter 4   "What can we do—religiously?"
The religion of peace   81
The Globalization of Creeds and Sects ❂
False Assumptions ❂ *The Globalization of
Wisdom and Symbols* ❂ *Religion after
September 11* ❂ *Toward Religious Freedom*

Conclusion: Freedom to Live in Peace   105

Appendix 1   Muhammad, Islam, Judaism,
                and Christianity   109

Appendix 2   A Guide to Further Reading   121

Index   123

The Author   131

Preface

I grew up in an intensely political household. Both my parents were politically active, and discussions on the issues of the day, in which my brothers and I were expected to participate, took place almost nightly around the dinner table. Although, as I reached adulthood, I became skeptical of my parents' political opinions, which could be described as state socialist, I remained keenly interested in politics, and my interest extended to economics. In due course I became a university professor in political economy, specializing in the history of economic ideas and in the relationship between the richer and the poorer countries of the world.

Like most left-wing intellectuals in the period following the Second World War, my parents were hostile to religion, especially Christianity. But in my teenage years, during the 1960s, I found myself, like many others of my generation, attracted to spiritual matters. I traveled extensively in India, studying Hindu thought, and also in the Muslim world, especially Afghanistan, where Sufism held a particular fascination. I then overcame inherited prejudice and turned my attention to Christianity. I spent a year in Ethiopia, the most ancient Christian country that was not subsequently conquered by Islam, where I immersed myself in Christian theology and mysticism. Eventually, I was ordained a Christian priest and became unpaid rector of an ancient church in a village near Cambridge, England. I have never subscribed to the notion that Christianity, or any other religion, has a monopoly on truth, and I continue to believe that in our spiritual journey we should take advantage of modern global communication by drawing wisdom from all religious traditions. Happily, after two decades, my congregation has come to share this openness, and I believe that, to some degree at least, the great majority of educated people in the West also share it. I should add that the present hierarchy of my denomination, the Church of England, is deeply suspicious; I am banned from preaching in several dioceses.

When, in the past, people have discovered that I have an academic and a personal interest in both politics and religion, they have generally been bemused, since in the popular mind these two spheres of human concern have come to be regarded in the West as quite separate. And when in books, lectures, and sermons I have made connections between the two, the reaction has sometimes been quite negative, particularly among persons of strong religious faith. But since September 11, 2001, all that has changed: no one can now doubt that, for good or ill, politics and religion are closely intertwined. So I find that, for the first time in my life, people are keen to explore how religion does, and should, influence politics, and how politics does, and should, influence religion.

On the evening of September 11, I was booked to speak at a religious meeting. Both my audience and I were reeling at the horror of what we had been witnessing on our television screens; clearly I had to cast aside my prepared address and offer a spontaneous response. Priests are expected to offer light and hope amid darkness and despair, and I found myself grappling with the possibility that this appalling event might somehow offer fresh opportunities to the world. I'm not sure that, at the time of my lecture, I really believed what I was saying; my thoughts were certainly a little jumbled. But during the following three days, an entire thesis formed in my mind that drew together ideas that I have held for many years. On September 14, with the encouragement and guidance of the British publisher John Hunt, I began to write this book, completing the first edition fifteen days later. The present edition contains some revisions, stimulated by the excellent editor at the American publishing house, Mike Ward.

I write as a scholar who respects the strict discipline of scholarship. I write as a teacher who enjoys making the fruits of scholarly endeavor accessible to students and the wider public. But, above all, I write as a person of deep and long-held convictions who wishes to persuade others of them. I hope that you may learn more about the subjects covered than you already know and that you will find the process of learning both easy and enthralling. But I also hope that you may come to think about these subjects in a different way than you did before. At the very least, I cherish the idea that you may engage in a mental debate with me.

In the weeks following September 11, amid the horror and grief, there was an intellectual earthquake: ideas were expressed, even by quite conservative writers, that would have seemed shockingly eccentric and even radical before that day. And although the earthquake has subsided, it has left the landscape of political and religious attitudes significantly different. The ideas expressed in this book, especially in chapters 3 and 4, were certainly eccentric prior to September 11, but now they seem far closer to the center of political and religious thinking.

There is nothing new in what I write; few authors can claim genuine originality. On matters of history, with which the first two chapters are mainly concerned, I rely on a wide variety of specialists, and the ideas of the last two chapters are drawn from great thinkers of the past. But I am bold enough to claim that some of the connections that I make, both historical and intellectual, are fresh. It is in these connections that any lasting value of this book lies.

In making such a claim, however, I must also make an apology — or, rather, a caveat. Although this book is suitable for students at colleges and universities, as well as for the wider public, it is not an academic tome, in which different historical judgments and shades of intellectual opinion are elucidated and balanced. Indeed, in order to illustrate the connections between diverse areas of thought and experience, it has been vital to paint each area with quite a broad brush. This has the added advantage of keeping the book short. But inevitably, there are specialists in each area who would take issue with me on particular matters. Therefore, I have indicated in the bibliography some excellent books in which the perspective is narrower and the brush finer.

A few years ago I was invited to speak at a ceremony celebrating the refurbishment of the main hall of the Boston Public Library. My great-great-great-grandfather, whose family had lived at Weymouth near Boston since 1635, founded the library in the nineteenth century. This wonderful institution, where any member of the public can enjoy freely one of the finest collections of books in the world, is a reminder both of America's idealism and of her unquenchable thirst for knowledge and understanding. Although I have lived in England for much of my life, I am an inheritor of American idealism and intellectual thirst. I hope this book is a worthy fruit of this inheritance.

Robert Van de Weyer, December 2001.

Introduction: Anguished Questions

Within hours of the planes' hurtling into the World Trade Center and the Pentagon on September 11, 2001, Americans were crying out in anguish, "Why do they hate us?" The question was echoed throughout Europe, since no one doubted that the attack was directed not just at America, but at the whole of western civilization.

It is a terrible question to ask because it suggests that the West may in some way be responsible, not for the atrocity itself, but for the conditions that motivated it. Yet the nature of the atrocity forces us to ask it. We can tighten our security, we can improve our intelligence, and we can deploy our most sophisticated weaponry. But most military experts tell us that, while such measures may inhibit terrorism, they can never overcome it. And we need only look to the conflicts between Israel and Palestine, between the Irish Republican Army (IRA) and Britain, and between Euzkadi ta Askatasuna [(ETA) Basque Fatherland and

Liberty] and Spain for confirmation of this glum progno-
sis. The British can cast their minds back into history for
further confirmation. In the heyday of their empire, when
their military might was unsurpassed, they frequently
suffered heavy casualties from Muslim warriors skilled in
the use of terror. On one occasion on the northwest fron-
tier of India, over two thousand women and children were
slaughtered in a single day, along with almost five thousand soldiers—a death toll similar to that of September 11.
The ultimate defeat of Islamic terrorism will only occur
when the well of hatred dries up, so that bright young and
wealthy older Muslims—modern terrorist warfare requires both great mental ability and substantial funds—
can no longer drink from it.

As we stare down that well, we see in its murky
waters thirteen centuries of rivalry between Islam and
Christianity, between the Muslim world and the Western
world. Within a century of Islam bursting out of the Arabian peninsula, Arab armies had subdued almost the
whole of Christendom and had only been halted in western France. A few centuries later European Christians
tried to take their revenge in the Crusades. Soon afterward Turkish Muslims were forcing their way into
Europe until they were stopped at Vienna. Then, through
a combination of capitalism and science, western Europe
became both rich and powerful, and, by the early twentieth century, most of the Muslim world was under direct
European rule. Today, although every Muslim country is
independent, western capitalism and science are more
dominant than ever. And just as Baghdad and, later,
Constantinople were the hubs of great Muslim empires,
so New York is the symbolic capital of the West. The

Islamic crusade against Western influence began two centuries ago in the Arabian desert, and Islamic militancy is now entrenched in most Muslim countries. Its primary targets have been the governments of those Muslim countries that the militants regard as too Western in both style and policy. But in recent decades, some militant groups have begun to turn their crusade of terror toward the West itself. There can be little doubt that, in the eyes of Islamic militants, the destruction of the World Trade Center was no more than an early victory in a long war.

Although enmity between Islam and the West goes back a long way, Muslims are not unique in trying to resist Western influence. Chinese resentment of the West flared up almost a century ago in the Boxer rebellion, in which large numbers of westerners were massacred. Gandhi's independence movement in India studiously avoided violence, but was no less determined. And we can find other movements, both bloody and peaceful, throughout Asia and Africa, in which local cultures have reasserted themselves. In recent years the growing movement against globalization has been founded on the conviction that unfettered Western capitalism, while making the West richer, has made much of the rest of the world poorer. Thus, while few people anywhere in the world approve the methods of Islamic terrorism, many people everywhere in the world understand the roots of Muslim resentment.

The first question about hatred begs a sequel: "Is mutual respect possible?" The answer is also to be found in history, and, happily, it is affirmative. Throughout the past millennium, there have been hugely fruitful exchanges between Islam and the West, in the sciences and medicine, in mathematics and astronomy, in the arts and philosophy, and most especially in religion and ethics—including the ethics of war. And both sides have gained in equal measure. Indeed, the European renaissance, in which modern Western life was born, would have been impossible without the influence of Islam, and Islam itself would have been impossible without Christianity. Thus we note that, although in the spheres of politics and economics Islam and the West are often in conflict, in knowledge and ideas they are often in harmony. And we must wonder whether this insight may have wider application: that, while political and economic globalization produces enmity across the world, intellectual globalization brings peace.

Now comes a third question, which is at the crux of our present dilemma: "What can we do to enable mutual respect to overcome hatred?" Even to pose this question is to risk Western indignation. Although anti-Islamic feelings lurk in some Western hearts, those feelings are surely trivial compared with the terrorists' loathing of the West. In that case, the primary responsibility for overcoming hatred, westerners may reasonably assert, lies within Islam. Yet if westerners have contributed to the conditions nurturing hatred, then westerners must contribute to the task of changing those conditions. And since in the present era the West is dominant, the West is best placed to begin the process of change. Moreover, self-protection demands it.

The history of conflict and harmony between Islam and the West suggests that this question must be answered at two levels: the economic and political, and the religious and moral. The West is rightly proud of its political freedom. But many in the West wrongly assume that political freedom also implies unfettered economic freedom, in which the market mechanism is supreme — a type of freedom symbolized by the World Trade Center. On the contrary, political freedom, which is based on democracy and the rule of law, implies that the people as a whole have the right and obligation to constrain the actions of individuals if they threaten the common good. This is a truth that Islam has well understood; indeed, the Muslim empires pioneered the notion of strong laws based on political consensus. In the present era, global peace depends on the political will to create a legal framework for global capitalism, so that all benefit, and on our understanding the true nature of the political freedom that we treasure so highly.

We do not need to know the identities of the hijackers, nor the name of the group to which they belonged, to realize that religion inspired them; only individuals motivated by the most fervent religious zeal could have gone willingly and deliberately to their own deaths in order to cause the deaths of thousands of others. And the understandable reaction of many westerners is to spit at religion itself, pointing not only to the present carnage but also to all the wars throughout history fought in the name of some religious creed. Yet human beings are innately religious, in that they wish to exert some degree of control over their inner selves and use symbols and rituals as means of achieving this. Although we cannot abolish religion, we must distinguish between good and bad religion — between those religions that nurture love and tolerance in the human psyche and those that nurture hate and bigotry. Both Islam and Christianity, in common with all the other major religions, have good forms and bad forms, and, undoubtedly, the form of fundamentalist Islam espoused by terrorists is disgustingly bad. In addition, in an age of global communication and intellectual skepticism, we must find religious forms that are plausible. Any kind of fundamentalism, in which some book or set of doctrines is deemed to encapsulate the truth, is wholly implausible. The search for good, plausible religion is ultimately our greatest challenge, but it offers our best hope for permanent peace.

"Why do they hate us?" "Is mutual respect possible?" "What can we do?" Chapters 1 and 2 of this book concern the first and second questions, respectively, and chapters 3 and 4 concern the third. Every religion contains the idea of good coming out of bad, and all of us in our personal lives have experienced numerous such instances. Great good may surely come out of the terrible evil of September 11. As we try to answer these three questions, we shall find ourselves addressing other problems, besides terrorism, besetting humanity, some of which pose an even greater threat to humanity's future. And in misty outline we shall discern a new political and religious order. If we start marching toward it, the thousands of victims of September 11 will not have died in vain.

Chapter 1

"Why do they hate us?" Islam and the West in conflict

The Arab Empire

Muhammad began to hear words, which he took to be divine revelations, in the year 610. These words were written down to form the Koran, the Islamic holy book. By the time of his death in 632, the prophet had united all the warring tribes of the Arabian peninsula under his leadership and convinced them of the truth of the Koran. During the following century, Arab warriors, inspired by the Koran, created an empire that spread across the Middle East, Iran, and Armenia to the borders of Afghanistan, and included the whole of North Africa, much of Spain, and Portugal. In 732, exactly a hundred years after Muhammad's death, the western advance of Islam was halted in France at Poitiers. But Islamic imperial power later spread eastward to the Indian subcontinent, and eventually, the whole of central Asia and much of southeast Asia also became Muslim.

The conquering Arabs had little doubt that they were fulfilling a divine plan, and that Allah was guiding them to victory. The peoples and nations subdued by them were mostly Christian; indeed, the Arab empire of the eighth century covered, with remarkable precision, the areas that had embraced Christianity. The Arabs were forbidden by the Koran from compelling Christians to embrace Islam; although they imposed a heavier tax on them, they otherwise allowed them to worship freely. Nonetheless, the majority of Christians in North Africa and the Middle East agreed with the Arab interpretation of events and converted. In this way, the original heartlands of Christendom became Muslim.

But the Christians of Europe, especially western Europe, remained more defiant. The reconquest of Spain by Christian forces began in earnest in the year 1000, and the Muslim rulers in parts of Italy and Sicily were driven out in 1061. In the Christian literature of western Europe Muhammad was vilified as an imposter driven by lust for power and women and was identified as the anti-Christ. Dante in *The Divine Comedy* consigned Muhammad to the lowest level of hell. The hatred of western Europeans for the Muslim infidel knew few bounds.

The Crusades

Muhammad visited Jerusalem as a young man, leading a caravan owned by the woman whom he later married. Jerusalem was the major trading center for goods from the Arabian peninsula, and Muhammad was impressed by both its cosmopolitan sophistication and its religious sites. In particular, the ruins of Solomon's temple, the Wailing Wall, imprinted itself on his imagination; years afterward, he dreamed of ascending in the temple a beautiful ladder, which led up to heaven—where he met Abraham, Moses, Aaron, and two cousins of Jesus. After his death, when the Arabs began their imperial adventures, Jerusalem was an early target, and it fell to them in 638. They then set about building a shrine, the Dome of the Rock, and a mosque, the al-Aqsa, near the Wailing Wall. But they left the churches and the Christian population unmolested, and they permitted the Jews, who had been banned from the city by the Christian rulers, to return.

The loss of Jerusalem was in itself of little consequence to Christians elsewhere, especially as the Muslim conquerors put no restrictions on Christian pilgrims visiting the city. Even in the eleventh century, as confidence among Christians in Europe began to return, the political status of Jerusalem remained largely a matter of indifference. However, in 1071, the Christian emperor of Constantinople, Romanus IV, whose empire had already been severely curtailed by Arab expansion, was captured and suffered a further heavy defeat at the hands of a new Muslim dynasty, the Seljuks, which also took control of Jerusalem at around this time. After many years of Turkic aggression, the Byzantines feared that the Seljuks would close the pilgrimage route to Jerusalem. So in the early 1090s, Byzantine Emperor Alexius Comnenus appealed to the pope in Rome and the Christian rulers of western Europe for support, proposing that they organize a military pilgrimage, with the purpose of protecting the route—and ultimately recapturing the holy city itself.

Pope Urban II saw such a military venture as an opportunity to heal the schism, which had occurred a few decades earlier in 1054, between the western (Catholic) and the eastern (Orthodox) church, bringing the whole of Christianity under papal rule. At the same time, European rulers were gaining in military strength, and several were attracted by the prospect of a pious campaign in which they might also establish permanent colonies in the Middle East. Meanwhile, European merchants were keen to maintain and strengthen lucrative commercial links. So, when Urban appealed for a crusade in 1095, political and commercial ambitions combined with religious zeal to produce a frenzy of enthusiasm. In 1099 the crusaders stormed Jerusalem, and for the first time in almost half a millennium, they brought it under Christian sovereignty.

The Christian hatred and resentment of Islam now had free rein. The crusaders systematically massacred the Muslims of the city, including women and children. They turned the Dome of the Rock into a church, converted the al-Aqsa mosque into a palace for a Christian king, and destroyed every other Muslim religious site. Similar massacres and desecrations occurred in other Middle Eastern cities, such as Antioch and Tyre, and in surrounding areas.

Christian rule in Jerusalem lasted less than a century. In 1187 a Muslim commander called Salah al-din—known as Saladin in the West—marched on the city. A story is told of a Christian preacher (usually identified as Waldes, later condemned as a heretic) going to Jerusalem and calmly walking out of the city to the Muslim encampment in order to speak to Saladin about Jesus Christ. Saladin received him warmly and acknowledged him as a worthy witness to Christ's love. But he added that, as a religion,

Christianity must be very feeble, since it had failed to restrain the crusaders' cruelty, while Islam by contrast enabled its adherents to maintain the highest moral standards. The preacher had no reply and returned to Jerusalem with his head bowed. When Saladin and his soldiers captured the city, their magnanimity seemed to prove his words: civilians were spared, and churches and shrines were left untouched.

The Ottoman Empire

At Muhammad's death, his father-in-law was appointed successor—caliph—to rule the Muslim community. And despite various disputes and schisms, most notably the separation of the Shiites in 662, there was a continuous line of caliphs ruling the Arab empire, initially from Damascus, and then from Baghdad. But by the thirteenth century, the empire had largely fragmented into a series of separate states, each ruled by its own sultan who paid the caliph only lip service. In 1258 the empire collapsed completely when a Mongol army, led by a grandson of Genghis Khan, captured Baghdad, burned the city and slaughtered the inhabitants, and executed the caliph and his family. For a few decades Mongol commanders ruled most of the Arab territories, although Egypt and Syria successfully resisted their attacks.

However, if Islam's enemies now felt more secure, their comfort was short-lived. Soon, three new Muslim empires arose and extended Islamic rule far beyond the original Arab dominions. Isfahan became the capital of a great Iranian empire, which spread northward into central Asia and eastward to include Afghanistan. Delhi became the capital of the Mughal empire, which included most of the Indian subcontinent. And Constantinople (modern Istanbul) became the center of the Ottoman empire—which soon began to threaten Christian Europe.

By the time Constantinople fell to the Ottomans in 1453, they had already assimilated most of Asia Minor, the area now called Turkey. Six years later they overran Serbia, and soon afterward, they conquered Bosnia. Early in the following century they incorporated much of Hungary. Their European advance was only halted in 1683— on September 11—when their siege of Vienna failed. Meanwhile, the Ottoman empire spread across North Africa, southern Russia, and Arabia, and Ottoman warships challenged Spain's naval supremacy. Once again, Muslims and their religion became objects of the deepest loathing and fear among Christians.

The Ottomans, whose ethnic origins remain a matter of dispute, were far more sophisticated in their political methods than the Arabs had been. The Arabs typically took over the existing political systems of the conquered lands, with the result that each area of their empire was ruled quite differently. Their main concern was to spread Islam and the Arabic language. This political diversity undoubtedly contributed to the Arab empire's eventual collapse. The Ottomans, by contrast, imposed their own centralized bureaucracy, whose main purpose was to impose and collect extremely heavy taxes. The revenue was then spent partly on military activity and partly on building some of the most magnificent palaces that the world had seen.

But like the Arab rulers, the Ottomans made no attempt to impose Islam by force. Indeed, their main religious concern was to prevent tension between the various religious groups within their empire. To this end, they organized a separate judicial system that incorporated the group's particular laws and customs for each religious group. And where members of different groups were living together in a single region, such as Bosnia, separate courts functioned side by side.

Western Imperialism

People traveling between the Christian and Muslim worlds at any time between the eighth and the seventeenth centuries were struck by the comfort and stability enjoyed by many Muslims, compared with the poverty, disease, and violence suffered by the majority of Christians. Most caliphs and sultans had a high regard for the law, and in general, they ruled fairly and justly; within the Arab and the Ottoman empires peace prevailed. Individuals could till the soil and ply their trades with little interference, to the benefit of all. Moreover, since the Muslim rulers prized every kind of scholarship, especially the sciences, there was steady progress in technology and medicine. By contrast, the kingdoms of Europe were frequently at war with one another, the feudal system of agriculture created little surplus to allow other trades to thrive, and the church was deeply suspicious of any kind of scientific endeavor.

But from the late seventeenth century on, the relative positions of the two worlds reversed with great rapidity. The Ottoman empire's heavy taxation discouraged enterprise, so the economy stagnated. And the Ottoman bureaucracy became hereditary, employing all the sons of existing officials, so it became both incompetent and bloated — requiring even heavier taxes to maintain. In northern Europe, however, a new class of energetic entrepreneurs arose, financed by bankers and investors who were willing to take considerable risks, and this capitalist spirit soon spread to southern Europe as well. At the same time, science broke free from its ecclesiastical shackles, and technology advanced with increasing speed. And the bitter religious and nationalistic Thirty Years' War convinced many rulers of the futility of war. Following the 1648 Peace Treaty of Westphalia, within Europe itself, a period of relative peace began, which lasted, with the notable interruption of the Napoleonic wars, for over two centuries.

Even before capitalism had begun to flourish, European sailors had already begun to erode Muslim dominance. Most notably, when Vasco da Gama rounded the southern tip of Africa in 1498 and continued onward to India, he broke the Muslim monopoly of the monsoon trade routes. (By cruel irony, his pilot was a great Muslim seafarer, Ibn Majid.) By 1508 the Portuguese were powerful enough to impose restrictions on trade between India and the Gulf. A century later, the Portuguese, the Dutch, and the British were competing in Southeast Asia over the valuable spice trade. To promote their own interests, they were each trying to establish colonial rule over Muslim kingdoms in that area.

But these were only the opening skirmishes in a process of economic and political conquest, whose extent and effects have far exceeded those of the Arabs and Ottomans combined, and capitalism was the main weapon. In 1603 the East India Company was formed by a group of English merchants, and soon it was forming military alliances with local Indian potentates, many of whom saw personal advantage in breaking away from Mughal rule. By the mid-nineteenth century, through the trading networks established by the East India Company, Indian farmers were producing vast amounts of raw cotton for the factories of northern England; factory owners exported the cloth back to India, undercutting the local spinners and weavers who had been central to rural prosperity. The Company was also involved in most other sectors of the Indian economy, remitting vast profits back to Britain. To protect its commercial interests, Company officials, protected by a highly efficient army, ruled directly or indirectly almost the entire subcontinent. After the Indian "mutiny" of 1857 was successfully put down, the last Mughal emperor was deposed, and the Company was replaced as the ruling power by the British government. Soon afterward, Queen Victoria was proclaimed Empress of India.

The colonization of India, in which commerce led and politics followed, became a model that all the main European powers followed throughout Asia and Africa, carving up the two continents between them. And since Islam was the dominant religion in much of Asia, almost all of North Africa, and a sizeable portion of sub-Saharan Africa, most Muslims found themselves under European rule. France concentrated on the western end of the Muslim world, occupying Algiers in 1830, and then gradually extending its control over the Sahara. In 1881 it occupied Tunisia. Three decades later, the Sultan of Morocco, still nominally independent, sought French support against Muslim insurgents within his own country. Spain, now feeling threatened by French power both to its north and to its south, reacted by occupying a chunk of western Morocco. Britain had already established a protectorate in Egypt, taking it out of Ottoman control. And in 1911, Italy decided to conquer the remaining Ottoman territories to the west of Egypt. Since the remnants of the Ottoman empire allied with Germany in the First World War, after Germany's defeat, the Ottoman's Muslim territories in the Middle East were divided between Britain and France, with Britain taking Palestine, Jordan, and Iraq, and France receiving Syria and Lebanon. By 1920, the only Muslim countries not under European control were Turkey, Afghanistan, Arabia, northern Yemen, and Iran; and Iran—or Persia, as it was then called—rapidly became a client state of Britain, who wished to protect its expanding oil company (the forerunner of BP) there.

Thus, the Islamic peoples who had once ruled and converted the heartlands of Christianity, and at various times had colonized large parts of Christian Europe, were now living under European domination.

The European empires of the nineteenth and early twentieth centuries were remarkably similar in their administration to the ancient Islamic empires, and just as Islamic rule had in many respects been benign, so was European rule. The European governments levied taxes on their colonies and provided political stability and a strong judicial system. They encouraged education and scholarship by establishing schools and colleges. They improved local transport by building roads and railways, which both helped the local economy and enabled their own troops to maintain order more efficiently. They urged charitable organizations to provide hospitals and clinics. And just as the Arab empire had made Arabic the common language, so each European power imposed its own language.

In two important respects, however, the European imperialists differed from their Muslim predecessors. First, the Europeans were secular; not only did they allow their subject peoples to practice their own religion but they also offered no incentive for them to adopt Christianity. They permitted Christian missionary societies to operate in Muslim territories, but they generally gave these societies no official support or blessing. And Muslims were free to organize their own missionary endeavors, both to resist Christian influence and to reach more remote groups that professed neither faith. By the nineteenth century, most Europeans regarded religion as a matter of personal and private choice that was unconnected with an individual's work or social status; and colonial policy reflected this attitude. As a result, in Muslim countries, Christian evangelism made virtually no impression — although in the non-Muslim areas of sub-Saharan Africa, it was more successful.

Secondly, the Europeans' primary interest was commercial: their troops and administrators provided a secure context for the expansion of European business. This commercialism was quite explicit in the case of the East India Company's colonization of India, and despite pious talk about "the white man's burden," financial rewards remained the main motive for every colonial venture. Thus, whereas the pattern of daily life remained virtually unchanged in the Muslim empires over many centuries, the economies of the European colonies were transformed within a few decades. Peasant farms producing subsistence crops declined, and large farms and plantations were laid out, producing cash crops for export. Traditional crafts were overwhelmed by imports from European factories; the surplus labor was employed in the extraction of raw materials for those factories. And while Europeans occupied the highest positions and took the bulk of the profits, local people soon rose to senior posts within European enterprises and often started their own businesses on Western lines. Thus, every European colony acquired a local westernized elite. In Muslim colonies most members of this elite grew away from their old religion, treating it as little more than a picturesque relic of the past.

In the two decades after the Second World War, the European empires were disbanded with remarkable speed and, in most cases, with little bloodshed. Indeed, in many cases, because the tax revenues had ceased to cover the growing costs of colonial rule, European leaders were happy to grant independence. The reins of government were quickly taken by the westernized elites; they in turn were committed to progress on Western lines—at an accelerating rate. Thus, to devout Muslims, who had watched the influence of their religion rapidly eroding, independence gave cause for even deeper despair, and this despair soon turned to anger.

Islamic Militancy

When the West began to assert itself economically and politically over the Muslim world, many Muslims interpreted their material inferiority as an indication that they had been lax in their religion and, hence, had incurred divine disapproval. In Arabia itself, in the mid-eighteenth century, the theologian al-Wahhab began a movement to revive the austere simplicity and rigorous discipline of early Islam. He joined forces with a tribal chief, Muhammad Ibn Saud, to drive out the Ottomans and bring most of the Arabian peninsula into a new Islamic state. (The dynasty founded by Ibn Saud is still in power in Saudi Arabia.) Other Muslim reformers urged cautious and gradual modernization in response to the West. In India, for example, Shah Wali Allah hoped to revive the fortunes of the crumbling Mughal empire by persuading Muslims to be more devout. But, rather than slavishly imitating the ancient past, he advocated adopting Western ideas and practices where they could be reconciled with the Koran.

But Western commerce and technology have their own power and momentum that are hard to check. By the mid-nineteenth century, it appeared to many Muslims that they either must become wholly westernized, or reject the West altogether; there was no middle way. The outstanding figure urging rejection was the wandering preacher, writer, and political activist al-Afghani. Born in Iran, he stirred up controversy in Afghanistan, Egypt,

India, Russia, France, Turkey, and Iran itself. Near the end of his life, the Iranian authorities who were hunting him down hanged three of his colleagues; he himself eluded the noose by dying of cancer. The heart of his message was that Islam was a comprehensive way of life, encompassing worship, law, government, and society. Therefore, it was utterly incompatible with any kind of Western, secular influence. It did not follow, however, that Muslims were condemned to technological backwardness. On the contrary, al-Afghani asserted, pointing to the great Islamic scientists of the medieval period, science was essentially a Muslim activity, which the West had appropriated. He urged Islamic countries to reject westernization in public and social life, and, at the same time, to learn Western science, in order to carry science forward themselves. Among Muslim governments, only the Ottomans made a serious attempt to encourage scientific endeavor, inviting westerners to found modern universities on their territory. But, since many of the westerners willing to respond were Christians, seeking to use the universities as a means of evangelism, science became associated in people's minds with Christianity—and so was discredited.

In the early decades of the twentieth century, in response to the Ottoman defeat in the First World War, the Muslim struggle against the West turned into a grassroots political and religious movement. In 1928 an Egyptian named Hasan al-Banna founded the Muslim Brotherhood, which rapidly spread across the Middle East; and a fellow Egyptian, Sayyid Qutb, supplied its uncompromising ideology. The Brotherhood attracted—and continues to attract—people from all social classes to form "families," which are brought together into groups; a number of groups then form a "battalion." Members are required to maintain strict personal and moral discipline and to meet regularly for prayer, athletic training is organized for the young men, and everyone has to engage in a program of Islamic education. Qutb taught that every Muslim government in the Middle East had been corrupted by Western ideas, and therefore must be overthrown. Governments committed to a rigid application of Islamic law—*sharia*—should be installed in their place. The Brotherhood has inspired numerous more fanatical offshoots, including the Egyptian Islamic Jihad (EIJ), whose most visible act was the assassination in 1981 of President Sadat of Egypt after he had signed the Camp David Accords with Israel's Menachem Begin, and opened Egypt up to Western investment. But the Brotherhood now permeates the armed forces and the civil service of most Muslim countries and has helped to push their governments toward the imposition of the *sharia*. And at every level of society it continues to inflame anti-Western emotions.

In Western eyes the two most spectacular victories for militant Islam have been the Iranian revolution in 1979 and the capture of Kabul by the Taliban in 1996. The Shah of Iran, and his father before him, tried to westernize their countries, banning Muslim dress in favor of Western styles, imposing laws that contradicted the *sharia*, and promoting Western forms of education. They also gave generous concessions to Western companies who invested in Iran. Whenever the Muslim clergy protested, the Shah reacted with contempt, referring to them as "black reactionaries." He expelled from the country the most vociferous protestor, Ayatollah Khomeini, but in exile, Khomeini proved far more dangerous. Aided by modern telecommunications, he rallied support and meticulously planned the Shah's overthrow. By the time Khomeini returned in triumph, even wealthy businessmen welcomed him. In deposing the Shah, Khomeini also hoped to depose all things Western, condemning America as "the great Satan."

The Taliban was originally a group of students, educated in the Wahhabist tradition in the madrassas (Islamic schools) of Pakistani refugee camps during the Afghan-Soviet war. In 1994, during the civil war that had followed Soviet withdrawal from Afghanistan, the Taliban began a military offensive to unite the warring nation with its vision of an Islamic state. After gaining power, the Taliban showed themselves to be even more rigorous than Khomeini in imposing the *sharia* — or rather, their interpretation of it, which many Islamic legal experts regard as crude and distorted.

In the meantime, there has been a resurgence of the original militant movement founded by al-Wahhab in Arabia. Although the Saudi dynasty was brought to power by his movement, no one imagines that the pampered princes of modern Arabia have the remotest interest in his teachings. But a new generation of Muslims, some in Arabia itself, see themselves as al-Wahhab's disciples, forming a network of organizations under a variety of names. They include the Algerian terrorists who, in trying to bring down the Algerian government, have killed tens of thousands of their compatriots; the Egyptian terrorists who, in 1997, killed seventy tourists in Luxor; the Kashmiri terrorists who, in striving to gain independence from India, kill innocent Hindus and Western travelers;

and, above all, Osama bin Laden and his al Qaeda group. Al-Wahhab himself authorized terrorist acts in his campaign to take over Arabia: in 1801 the Wahhabis slaughtered two thousand ordinary citizens in the streets of Qarbala. His modern followers have long surpassed his grisly record.

While the relative poverty of the Middle East in relation to the West has been the spur to militancy, it is not poverty itself that drives individuals to become militants. On the contrary, many leading militants are from relatively wealthy families, and many have even received Western-style education. For them the Middle East's economic problems are a source of humiliation, and hence an affront to their faith. Their knowledge of the West only serves to deepen this inner wound. Waging war on the West is a means of restoring their self-respect.

Zionism

Although there were Jewish communities throughout the Middle East and southern Europe at the time of Christ — Paul's missionary journeys were mainly aimed at them — the number of Jews living away from their historic homeland was greatly increased after the Jewish rebellion against Roman occupation, which culminated in the siege and fall of Jerusalem in 70 C.E. Thus, in the time of Muhammad, there were groups of Jews in the major Arabian cities, mostly engaged in trade. Muhammad acquainted himself with their religion, which he held in very high regard. And when he received the words of the Koran, he saw himself as another prophet on the Jewish model—a spiritual descendant of Abraham, Moses, Elijah, Isaiah, and the rest. Therefore, he expected the Jews of Arabia to support him in his quest to call the Arabian people to faith in God. But, according to the authoritative accounts of Muhammad's life, the Arabian Jews refused to accept him as a prophet, and they mocked his religious teaching as crude and naïve. Despite his deep disappointment, he refused to condemn or persecute them, and his belief in the fundamental unity of Islam and Judaism was undimmed. This tolerant and respectful attitude toward Jews and their faith remained the norm among Muslims for thirteen centuries, and most major Muslim cities had Jewish communities that peacefully prospered.

But in the twentieth century, with the rise of Zionism, rooted in a Western interpretation of Judaism and supported by Western money and weapons, tolerance turned into hatred and respect into contempt. And as we enter the twenty-first century, Zionism is a central focus of Muslim enmity toward the West.

The origins of Zionism lie in a strange combination of German nationalism, Jewish prosperity, Christian zeal, and anti-Semitism. Throughout the nineteenth century, as western European societies became more secular in outlook, Jews were assimilated, ceasing to form separate groups, and many rose to great prominence in commerce, politics, the arts, and the sciences. Some, like the fathers of the British prime minister Benjamin Disraeli and the social philosopher Karl Marx, abandoned the Jewish faith altogether and, for largely social reasons, received Christian baptism. Others remained loyal to Judaism, regarding it as a purely spiritual bond that was entirely compatible with patriotism toward their country. Nowhere was the assimilation more complete than in Germany. Yet, the unification of Germany helped to stimulate a fervent sense of German nationhood and, in the minds of some, a sense of German racial superiority. This had a double effect on German Jews. On the one hand, it awakened in them a sense of their own distinct national and racial identity; on the other, it made them feel uncomfortable and unwelcome within Germany.

The success of Jews within Western societies, and especially their scientific and artistic eminence, also reawakened their view of themselves as a messianic people, called by God to be a sign of social justice, universal prosperity, and permanent peace. And the messianic vision could only be realized within the Jews' historic home: Jews must return in large numbers to Palestine and create a perfect society in accordance with the Law and the Prophets. As Moses Hess wrote in 1862 in a book provocatively entitled *Rome and Jerusalem,* "It is only with a national rebirth that the religious genius of the Jews, like the giant of the legend touching Mother Earth, will be endowed with new strength and again be inspired with the prophetic spirit." Not only did many of Hess's fellow Jews respond with enthusiasm, but so also did a small, but influential, number of Christians. The earl of Shaftesbury in England, renowned as a social reformer and the leader of the evangelical movement within the Church of England, regarded the return of Jews to

Palestine as the fulfillment of prophecies within the New Testament. He was the first of numerous Evangelical Christians, in Britain and America, to give their fervent support to the Zionist cause.

Initially, Jews advocating a return to Palestine envisaged a cluster of agricultural settlements, with some adjoining workshops in which ancient crafts would be practiced. They also imagined a few cultural and religious centers, which Jews and Gentiles from across the world could visit for inspiration. From the 1870s, small groups of Jews from western Europe and Russia began purchasing land from Palestinians, with money from both Jewish and Christian benefactors. In 1883, the hugely wealthy Jewish banker Baron Edmond de Rothschild of Paris began pumping much larger amounts into the establishment of these Jewish colonies. However, this essentially religious movement turned political through the tireless advocacy of Hungarian journalist Theodor Herzl, the "father of Zionism." By the 1890s, German and Austrian nationalism was starting to express itself in strong antipathy to Jews and to the economic privileges they had won for themselves; moreover, the Dreyfus affair in France showed that anti-Semitism was spreading. Herzl concluded that permanent assimilation of Jews into European life was impossible, and in 1896, he published a pamphlet, *The Jewish State,* in which he proposed forming a new Jewish nation in Palestine. In a novel published six years later he depicted this nation as a kind of Jewish version of a western European state, a Hebrew Vienna. A follower of Herzl coined the name "Zionism" for Herzl's vision—Zion, being the hill in Jerusalem where King Solomon built the temple.

In the early years of the twentieth century, the flow of Jews to Palestine increased rapidly to about 90,000 by 1914; the flow of money from wealthy Jews remaining in Europe rose in proportion. In 1917 the leaders of the Zionist movement achieved their first major political victory: they persuaded the British government to declare its support publicly for "the establishment in Palestine of a national home for the Jewish people." The only Jew in the British cabinet was opposed to this declaration, expressing the fear that involving Judaism in politics would corrupt its spiritual purity, compromise its message, and, worst of all, be a further spur to anti-Semitism. Although his unease about Zionism was now felt by a growing number of European Jews, his Christian colleagues overruled him.

When, in the aftermath of the First World War, Britain took control of Palestine, Zionist hopes rose. British policy in Palestine, however, was confused. To enable the establishment of a Jewish national home, the British authorities encouraged Jewish immigration. Within a decade, the Jewish population in Palestine tripled, and the area of Palestine owned by Jews also multiplied. The authorities also allowed the Jews to build an entire city, Tel Aviv, as the center of Jewish industry and commerce. But the declaration of 1917—known as the Balfour Declaration, after the devoutly Christian foreign secretary who wrote it—deliberately stopped short of advocating a Jewish state, and it contained the proviso that "nothing shall be done which may prejudice the civil and religious rights of existing non-Jewish communities in Palestine." The British authorities strived to ensure peaceful coexistence between the Muslim Palestinians and the Jewish settlers, hoping that, in due course, the two groups would come together to form a single independent state. Indeed, peaceful coexistence had also been Herzl's dream.

But it soon became clear that a Jewish national home and the upholding of Palestinian rights were incompatible — as wise heads had predicted. And the British found themselves caught between Jew and Arab, taking the brunt of both sides' anger. The Palestinian Arabs feared that a Jewish state, in which they would be second-class citizens, was the inevitable consequence of unrestricted Jewish immigration. Several times after 1929 they organized revolts, which the British suppressed. Eventually, in 1939, the British government acknowledged Palestinian grievances by limiting Jewish immigration to 15,000 people per year. Militant Jews responded by mounting a terrorist campaign against the British, culminating in the bombing in 1946 of the King David Hotel in Jerusalem, which contained British administrative and military offices; ninety-one people were killed. The militants also organized illegal immigration.

Hitler, through his efforts to exterminate the Jews in Europe, ensured their success in Palestine. Such was the horror and the guilt felt by Europeans at the Holocaust, as the full extent of it became clear, that the British and other European governments no longer felt able to resist Jewish demands. Besides, Jewish terrorism had worn down British resolve. In 1948 the British withdrew, leaving the UN to partition the territory into a Jewish and an Arab state.

The Legacy

Imperial rulers may treat their subjects with tolerance and even kindness. The Muslim empires stretching into Europe in medieval times were commendably tolerant toward both Christians and Jews and were occasionally benevolent. The European empires of the recent past, stretching across the historic lands of Islam, were also tolerant; many European governors and administrators, often motivated by Christian faith, made great efforts to improve the lives of their subjects. But when people of one culture and religion rule by force those of a different culture and religion, there is, inevitably, a legacy of deep bitterness.

The additional and crucial twist for Muslims is that, while the Western empires have been dismantled, Western dominance persists and grows. When the Arabs, and later the Ottomans, withdrew from Christian Europe, they played no further part in European life. As a result, the bitterness of occupation could gradually lessen, and Europe's memory of the economic and cultural superiority of Islam could fade. But since the Muslim countries gained their political freedom, Western goods, Western investment, and the Western media have actually become more, not less, important. Muslims are reminded day by day, hour by hour, of their economic inferiority to, and dependence on, the West. They watch and enjoy Hollywood movies, and admire and envy the American way of life portrayed in them, but they resent their own inability to provide such a way of life for themselves.

The strength of Zionism both symbolizes and accentuates the Muslim dilemma. Israel is an astonishing economic success: it has made deserts bloom, created thriving industries from nothing, and in recent years has been among the leaders in technological innovation. With American arms, it has formed an army that on three occasions has defeated the combined forces of its Arab neighbors, extending its borders in the process. In Arab eyes, Israel is a chunk of the West, in all its material glory, transplanted in their territory—which is precisely how the early Zionists envisaged it. Almost every Arab sympathizes with the plight of the Palestinians, confined to a small segment of their former homeland. In a recent poll over 60 percent of respondents in Saudi Arabia, Kuwait, the Emirates, and Lebanon, and almost 80 percent of Egyptians, answered that Palestine is "the single most important issue to them personally." But the hatred of Zionism is also a proxy for Arab emotions toward the entire Western world—and especially America.

Yet Israel is a profoundly flawed symbol of the West, and its flaw causes Muslims, to some degree, to misunderstand the West, adding to their resentment. The founding fathers of the United States were passionately secular; they wanted a clear separation between politics and religion and enshrined this in the Constitution. The nations of western Europe have almost become secular, although a few, like Britain, retain nominal Christian links. Indeed, in the days following September 11, both President George W. Bush in America and Prime Minister Tony Blair in Britain emphasized that the West was not at war with Islam as such and urged their people to treat their Muslim compatriots with respect.

The state of Israel, by contrast, is founded on a particular religion, Judaism, and seeks to embody its religion's values. It continues to receive financial aid and moral approval from Jews in America and western Europe, and also from a certain type of evangelical Christian. Indeed this combination of Jewish and Christian devotion to Israel has virtually compelled American governments to continue supplying military aid to the Israeli army. Thus, for many Arabs, the existence of Israel gives their resentment of the West a more pronounced, and largely unjustified, religious dimension.

Throughout the twentieth century, Islamic militancy was mainly directed toward the governments of Muslim countries for adopting policies influenced by Western ideas. At the start of the twenty-first century, Islamic militancy is turning toward the sources and promoters of those ideas.

Chapter 2

"Is mutual love and respect possible?" *Islam and the West in harmony*

Christian Roots of Islam

On his journey to Jerusalem, leading his future wife's caravan, Muhammad stopped in the shade of a tree that happened to be near the cell of a Christian monk. The monk emerged from his cell and engaged Muhammad in conversation. The monk was deeply impressed by the young Muhammad's natural wisdom and prophesied that he would be a messenger of God. Some time later, at Muhammad's wedding, Muhammad's assistant recalled this incident to one of Muhammad's cousins, who was a Christian renowned for the depth of his scholarship. The Christian scholar was inclined to believe the monk's prophecy; he added that he had become weary of waiting for God's messenger and was now greatly relieved that he had arrived.

These incidents are recalled in a book compiled a few decades after Muhammad's death by the historian Ibn Ishaq, who collected oral and written accounts of Muhammad's life and arranged them in chronological order. The incidents convey the importance of Christianity in Muhammad's religious formation. By Muhammad's time, Christian monasticism was at its height, and there were tens of thousands of hermits, and many hundreds of monastic communities, scattered across the deserts of the Middle East. Among these Christian ascetics, many were recognized as prophets, enjoying direct communication with God; in the surviving monastic literature of this period, God frequently speaks. Thus, when Muhammad went out night after night into the hills north of Mecca, he would not have been surprised to hear those divine utterances, later dictated to a scribe, that formed the Koran. And since Muhammad in his youth relished conversations about religion, it is reasonable to suppose that he had many long discussions about Christianity with his Christian cousin.

In the Koran itself, the birth and miracles of Jesus are recounted, and he is acknowledged as a great prophet. The Koran contains many ideas that were current in the Christian theology of Muhammad's time. In particular, it speaks of a day of resurrection in which the dead will be brought back to life, and it emphasizes time and again that this resurrection will be bodily, with the dead emerging from their graves. At this moment, God will pass judgment, casting the wicked into a fiery hell, and directing the righteous to eternal paradise. The Koran denies the divinity of Jesus, saying that all prophets are human beings whom God has chosen, and it denies that the crucifixion ever occurred, thereby refuting any notion that the death of Jesus was a sacrifice for human sin. But there were many Christians in Muhammad's time, Arians and Gnostics respectively, whom other Christians condemned as heretics, who also denied these things. Thus, the theology of the Koran may be regarded as a heretical form of Christianity, and Muslims as those who treat the Arian and Gnostic heresies as orthodoxy.

A further incident in the early history of Islam reveals the degree to which Muslims respected and trusted Christians and the initial unity between them. The Muslim community initially faced vicious opposition from the tribal leaders in Mecca, including several attempts to murder Muhammad himself. Although Muhammad himself remained in Mecca, he sent some of his followers to Ethiopia, a Christian country, for protection. The Ethiopian king received them warmly and invited them to his court to speak about Muhammad and his message. The king and the Christian bishops who were in attendance were deeply impressed by what they heard and declared that Muhammad was indeed a divine messenger.

Philosophy and Theology

In 641 the Arabs conquered Alexandria. Several centuries earlier, this beautiful city on the Egyptian coast had taken over from Athens as the main center of philosophical thought. Numerous academies had been founded there, in which the style of intellectual inquiry pioneered by Plato and Aristotle was continued with untiring vigor. And from the third century onward, it had also become a major center of Christian theology. Men such as Origen and Clement, who combined fierce intelligence with mystical insight, used the ideas of Plato, in particular, to develop a Christian understanding of humanity's relationship with divinity. Thus, less than a decade after Muhammad's death, his followers—mostly illiterate warriors from the remote Arabian desert—were breathing the air of one of the most sophisticated cultures that the world had seen.

They were invigorated by it. When the Arabs established their capital in Baghdad, the caliph immediately invited philosophers from throughout his empire to join him there. He built houses for them as well as halls in which they could give lectures and hold debates. Some of these philosophers subscribed to no religion, but many were Christian and some were Jewish; anyone of intellectual ability and deep scholarship was welcome. The caliph's recruitment campaign was helped in the middle of the sixth century by the decision of the Christian emperor in Constantinople to banish all philosophers from his empire, even Christian ones, on the grounds that philosophical discussion was incompatible with Christian belief. Most of the exiled philosophers took refuge in Iran, where the king was sympathetic. As Iran was absorbed into the Arab empire, the intellectual descendents of these refugees eagerly moved to Baghdad.

Since they spoke and wrote in a variety of different languages, the first task was to establish communication between the philosophers. Naturally, the caliph ordered that Arabic should be the common language. As a result, not only did the philosophers themselves have to master Arabic but also every philosophical work of merit had to be translated into Arabic. Throughout the eighth century, many of the great texts of Greek philosophy, including those of Aristotle and Plato, plus several works in Syriac, were rendered into the language of the Koran. And so broad were the intellectual interests of the Arab rulers that at least one Hindu work, composed in Sanskrit, was also translated.

Islamic philosophy now entered a golden age. In due course, the writings of its leading philosophers were to exert a global influence, most especially in Christian Europe. Four philosophers stand out. The first was al-Razi, born in about 865, who was trained in medicine and for much of his life worked as a physician and hospital administrator. But he wrote at least two philosophical works, one on ethics, *Spiritual Medicine,* and the other, *Philosophic Life,* on the relationship between religion and philosophy. While acknowledging the importance of prophets like Muhammad, he believed that all religious and ethical truth could be directly attained by the human mind through rational contemplation. In order to engage in such contemplation, the mind must free itself from all passion and emotion, and thus become utterly objective. The essence of truth, as the mind finally discerns, is pure love, whose outward expression is "to treat all people justly." Al-Razi recommended that individuals desiring emotional liberation should have a personal teacher to guide them and condemned all kinds of religious groups whose laws required them to behave unjustly, or to behave justly only toward other members of their group. Pure love, he taught, is universal.

Ibn Sina—known in the West as Avicenna—lived about a century later. He grappled with three theological issues that have equally dogged Islam and Christianity. The first is the existence of evil. He argues that, as creator of the world, God must be responsible for the evil within it: "If only pure righteousness prevailed in the world, it would be a different world from the one God made." This leads him to the second issue, the notion of reward and punishment. He argues that God has inserted in the human soul a tendency toward goodness, in that good acts bring peace to the soul, whereas bad acts bring turmoil. These inner feelings experienced during earthly life, rather than in heaven or hell after death, are the true consequences of our moral choices. And this leads to the third issue — the nature of religious language. He acknowledges that prophets have to use stark and simple images in order to convey their message to the common people, but says that the reflective person should regard these as images and metaphors of the truth, rather than the truth itself. Among these metaphors he includes not only heaven and hell, but also resurrection and prayer. The resurrection of the body, taught by the Koran, indicates that life continues beyond death. In fact, only the soul survives — a notion that, in Avicenna's eyes, is too subtle for most human beings to comprehend. Praising God and making requests, which are the outward forms of prayer, are really vehicles enabling individuals to align their wills with that of God.

In the early part of his life, al-Ghazali, who lived in the eleventh century, put forward a vigorous defense of a literal interpretation of the Koran, giving reasons for believing in the bodily resurrection and in heaven and hell. He also argued that if philosophers pursue reason alone as the means of ascertaining the truth, they must ultimately destroy religion and morality. But, according to his autobiography, he gradually grew weary of both philosophy and theology, since they are merely verbal discussions about God. Instead, he longed to encounter God face to face. So, after much hesitation, he decided to train as a mystic: he gave away his wealth, went to live in solitude, and devoted himself to meditation. After ten years, he achieved his goal and experienced a state of certainty and ecstasy. Al-Ghazali's spiritual journey was echoed two centuries later in Paris by Thomas Aquinas, the greatest Christian theologian of medieval times, who was deeply influenced by Islamic thought. Toward the end of his life, he too had a mystical experience, after which he wrote, "Such things have been revealed to me that all I have written seems like straw."

Ibn Rushd, known in the West as Averroes, was born in Cordoba, Spain, in 1126 and became a judge in his home city. The sultan of Morocco later invited him to be his physician and personal adviser. Whereas al-Razi and Avicenna took their inspiration from Plato, Averroes was a follower of Aristotle, writing a masterly commentary on his works. Like Francis Bacon half a millennium later, Averroes argued that, since science is essentially a religious activity, scientific inquiry should be free from religious dogma. By studying creation as it is, the scientist is uncovering the mind of the creator. Like many modern Western theologians, he argued that there are many sources of religious insight—natural beauty, dialectical argument, poetry and literature—and that all are equally valid. And like many medieval Christian writers, such as Bernard of Clairvaux, he believed that Scriptures must often be interpreted allegorically.

Throughout the early medieval period—the so-called Dark Ages—there was little interest among Christian Europeans in philosophical matters, and the old Latin translations of Aristotle's works, many of Plato's works, and those of other ancient Greek philosophers were lost. But by the twelfth century, universities were beginning to flourish in a few European cities, and the proximity of Muslim Spain stimulated more adventurous Christian scholars to learn Arabic and thereby acquaint themselves with Islamic ideas. And as they studied the Muslim philosophers, they were led to the Greek sources that inspired them. Michael the Scot and Herman the German led the way in translating the works of Plato and Aristotle from Arabic into medieval Latin. They also translated the works of the leading Muslim philosophers themselves, in particular Avicenna and Averroes. The effect on European thought was startling. Christian theology burst into life, with theologians reworking the whole of Christian doctrine in the light of Greek philosophy. In his monumental *Summa Theologiae*, Thomas Aquinas, in the thirteenth century, founded his method of argument on Aristotle's system of logic and his theology itself on Aristotle's philosophical categories and concepts. Aquinas quarreled with Averroes' interpretation of Aristotle's ideas. In the University of Paris, of which Aquinas was a member, theologians divided into the so-called Latin Averroists and those who followed Aquinas's line. The conflict between the two groups became so fierce that the bishop of Paris eventually had to intervene, coming down on Aquinas's side. The Aristotelian theology of Thomas Aquinas remains the basis of Roman Catholic orthodoxy, and even today, men training for the Catholic priesthood have to study his writings.

In due course, Europeans made translations of Plato and Aristotle directly from the original Greek, and, by the sixteenth century, few European writers referred by name to Avicenna and Averroes. But no historian of ideas disputes the continuing indirect influence of these great Muslim philosophers. Indeed, even when the Protestant reformers tried to turn their backs on philosophy itself—Luther referred to it as "vanity and perdition"—their own styles of argument and even their ideas owe an unconscious debt to Islam. The Protestant elevation of the Bible into the "Word of God" is almost identical to al-Ghazali's understanding of the Koran. And subsequent debates in Protestant churches about biblical interpretation, with those favoring a literal approach opposed by those who see many biblical stories as metaphors and myths, echo Muslim debates about how the words of the Koran should be understood. In the longer run, the more profound Muslim influence on European thought was in liberating it from religious dogma. For Avicenna and Averroes, spiritual devotion and intellectual inquiry, far from being opposed, complemented one another. Indeed, for Averroes, unrestrained scientific investigation was actually a religious obligation. The European renaissance, and all that flowed from it, would have been impossible without the winds of freedom that blew from the world of Islam.

Science, Mathematics, and Medicine

In 1575 the Ottoman emperor set up an observatory in Constaninople. In a painting that survives of its operation, every kind of scientific instrument is visible: set squares and protractors, a theodolite and an astrolabe, a spirit level and a clock, a weighing machine using springs, and an optical device that appears like a microscope. There is also a globe whose depiction of the continents seems quite accurate. It was at least a century before Europe had anything to match this remarkable establishment, and without the pioneering work of Muslim scientists and mathematicians, the scientific revolution in Europe would have taken far longer.

The painting of the Constantinople observatory illustrates a wider point: that science was integral to the social and political ideology of the Islamic empires. The caliphs in Baghdad believed that their empire incorporated most of the civilized world—they were unaware of how vibrant was the civilization of China. And they saw Islam as the inheritor and guardian of all human knowledge, including mathematics and the natural sciences, with a divine responsibility to push forward the frontiers of knowledge. To fulfill this responsibility, they arranged for scientific works from every region of the empire, and beyond, to be translated into Arabic, just as they had organized the translation of philosophical works. Scholars familiar with Greek and Latin, Persian, Syriac, and Sanskrit, were recruited for this task. (The most famous of these translators, fluent in at least three languages, was a Christian named Hunayn.) They also encouraged young men of scientific inclination to do fresh research and write new works and provided whatever facilities they required.

As in ancient Greece, the greatest field of scientific interest was astronomy. As early as 830, Muslim astronomers had produced comprehensive tables for the movements of the sun, the moon, and the planets, using mathematical calculations derived from both Indian and Greek sources. But soon, these calculations were shown to be flawed, so new methods of calculation had to be found. This led to the development of trigonometry and various other mathematical tools. The most distinguished Islamic astronomer, Ibn al-Shatir, who lived in the fourteenth century, produced a series of mathematical models that were reproduced a century and a half later by Copernicus. There is reason to think that al-Shatir concluded from these models, as Copernicus did, that the earth was not stationary, but moved round the sun.

Within the sphere of mathematics itself, the Muslims adopted the Indian counting system, with the base ten, and they adapted the Indian numerals, enabling any number to be denoted using only nine digits and zero. When, many centuries later, Europe began using these numerals in place of the cumbersome Roman letters, they had the grace to acknowledge their debt by referring to them as "Arabic numerals." In the early ninth century, a Muslim genius named al-Khwarizmi invented an entirely new mathematical discipline, algebra. In doing so, he showed how algebraic equations, both linear and quadratic, provide an abstract means of solving a wide range of practical problems. A few decades later, other mathematicians were demonstrating how algebra may be applied to the branch of mathematics in which the ancient Greeks had excelled, geometry, even suggesting that geometry should be subsumed within algebra. Century after century, further new mathematical concepts were developed, including negative and real numbers, decimal fractions, and general algorithms in the theory of equations. In the eleventh century, a mathematician named al-Haytham wrote a book applying many of these concepts to optics, which found its way into Europe and became the standard work on the subject until the seventeenth century. A later Muslim expert in optics, Farisi, explained the rainbow.

Muslim engineers concentrated their main efforts on the extraction, use, and distribution of water. They built underground conduits to carry water from aquifers to centers of population, thereby minimizing loss through evaporation. They built dams both for irrigation and for providing waterpower with which to drive mills. They invented complex water-raising machines to place over wells. And they built elegant bridges with water mills attached to their piers. They also worked with architects and artists to create mosques and palaces of breathtaking elegance and beauty.

Muslim physicians had the benefit of Arab translations of both ancient Greek texts, such as the works of Hippocrates, and Indian texts describing the Ayurvedic system; many of their remedies were derived directly from these sources. However, al-Razi and Avicenna, respectively, made two advances in medical methodology that laid the foundations for modern Western medicine. Al-Razi ran a hospital in which he pioneered experimental research. To test each remedy, he divided his patients into two groups, one of which received the remedy and the other did not; he then observed and tabulated the results. The most famous work emerging from these experiments was a monograph on the treatment of smallpox and measles, which guided European physicians until the eighteenth century. Avicenna, prompted by Aristotle's work on the subject, realized that a proper understanding of human anatomy was vital in the development of new treatments, and he made the first systematic study of the human body.

Politics and Law

When people speak of the principles on which Western political systems rest, they typically mention democracy and the rule of law. Democracy, in the words of Abraham Lincoln, ensures that government is "of the people, by the people, and for the people." The rule of law enables citizens to know clearly their obligations to society and to understand the sanctions they will incur if they fail to fulfill those obligations. Together, democracy and the rule of the law save people from the arbitrary whims of dictators and tyrants and make all citizens politically equal. Democracy was pioneered by ancient Athens; Moses and the ancient Hebrews introduced the rule of law in a tribal context; and Muslims extended it as the central principle of national and imperial government.

From the outset, Islam was a political religion. Muhammad was not only a prophet, but also a charismatic political leader, and when he died, the caliphs succeeding him took over his political—but not his prophetic—role. At first, the caliphs, assisted by advisers, made decisions as new problems and issues arose, and they appointed judges to enforce their decisions and to settle disputes. But while people had trusted that Muhammad's decisions were divinely guided, they had less trust in the caliphs. And as the Muslim territories expanded, absorbing regions with quite different customs and traditions than those of the Arabian peninsula, judges were uncertain as to what extent local traditions should influence their rulings. It soon became clear that a unified body of laws was required that would guide—and constrain—both the caliphs and the judges. By the eighth century, in several of the major cities of the empire, there were legal scholars striving to formulate an Islamic legal code, and by the year 900, the highly sophisticated system of law known as the *sharia* was in place throughout the Muslim world.

According to al-Shafii, a scholar from Mecca who is commonly recognized as the father of Islamic jurisprudence, the law should have four roots. The first is divine revelation in the Koran. The Koran condemns particular practices, such as murder, theft, usury (charging interest on loans), exploitation of the poor, false contracts, and adultery; according to al-Shafii, these practices should be illegal. The Koran also strongly advises against certain forms of behavior, such as drinking alcohol and gambling, and al-Shafii argues that this advice should also be enshrined in law. In addition, the Koran indicates a certain ethical bias. For example, while not banning slavery, it urges slave owners to free their slaves; though not banning polygamy, it orders men to limit the number of their wives to four; and while permitting divorce, it indicates a strong preference for lifelong unions. Al-Shafii's writings, and those of later jurists following his lead, show how these ethical biases can be applied in law with subtlety and discretion, putting such a price on slavery and polygamy that they disappear of their own accord.

The second root of the law, according to al-Shafii, is the *sunna*, the words and deeds of Muhammad. Although, according to the Koran itself, Muhammad was a fallible human being, God chose him as a prophet for his wisdom and insight, and so his recorded sayings and his personal example indicate how human beings should live. The *sunna* in turn revealed the third root of law. Muhammad said, "My community will never agree on an error." Al-Shafii interpreted this as meaning that, when a general consensus forms that some particular type of behavior is right or wrong, this consensus should be legally binding on individuals. The fourth root is analogical reasoning from the other three roots: some antisocial actions, not included in the other three roots, may be deemed illegal if they are similar in essence to actions that are included.

Although the Koran is the primary source of Islamic law, legal scholars have always recognized that legal matters comprise only a small portion of it; the main themes of the Koran are basic religious and moral principles. Scholars have also recognized that the teachings of the Koran in certain parts were connected with the particular circumstances of the time and place in which they were revealed. Indeed, the Koran was given to Muhammad gradually over twenty-three years, and some of its contents were explicit responses to events that occurred during that period. Thus, from al-Shafii onward, legal scholars have sought to distill from the Koran the ethical rules that are immutable and that should, therefore, form the overriding objectives of the *sharia*. But they have allowed for the possibility that the means of fulfilling these objectives may evolve according to changing needs and experience. The overriding objectives are generally held to be the promotion of fairness, equality, prosperity, and human dignity, the establishment and maintenance of a government that consults the people, the prevention of injury, the removal of hardship, and moral education. An example of the evolution of the *sharia* concerns the treatment of teachers. Originally, religious teachers were banned from charging fees, as teaching was regarded as an act of spiritual merit, but when too few people offered themselves for this task, modest fees were permitted.

In the heyday of Islamic power, the *sharia* was regarded by Muslims as one of the chief blessings of their religion, and it was the envy of foreigners who visited Muslim lands. But in recent decades, as independent Muslim states have tried to reimpose the *sharia,* virtually all outsiders, and most ordinary Muslims, have been horrified. The problem is that many Muslim politicians and activists today appear ignorant of the third and fourth of al-Shafii's roots. For example, the Taliban in Afghanistan formulated a legal code that claimed to be based on the Koran and the sayings of Muhammad, without reference to popular consensus or to rational argument. Al-Shafii well understood that the Koran and the *sunna* are open to widely varying interpretations. Hence, consensus and reason are necessary to ensure that interpretations are wise and humane. The Taliban demonstrated that, when consensus and reason are abandoned, the overriding objectives of the *sharia,* far from being fulfilled, are cruelly frustrated.

Warfare

When Muhammad began his prophetic mission, he saw himself only as a teacher, passing on to his compatriots what God had told him. Then, as the leaders of his own tribe turned against him and his followers, making several attempts on his life, it became clear that Islam would only survive by means of military victory. Ibn Ishaq's biography of Muhammad records the moment when God gave Muhammad permission to call his followers to arms. Until that moment, God had required Muhammad "to endure all the insults thrown at him, and to forgive the ignorance of those who rejected his call ... while the tribal leaders were free to persecute Muslims without fear of retribution." From the outset, Muhammad had taught his followers that Islam involved a spiritual *jihad* in which they must wage war on the evil inclinations within themselves. Now they were free to wage a physical *jihad* against those who upheld evil in the world.

But this divine permission was not without stringent conditions. "First," according to Ibn Ishaq's account, "God ordered Muslims to fight only those who persecuted them for their faith; they should not make war for the sake of gaining power and wealth. Secondly, they should never use deceit in conducting warfare, but should fight honestly. God also commanded that, when they achieve victory, Muslims should not exploit those whom they have vanquished; their only aims should be to enable Islam to be practiced fully and freely, and to ensure that people live in peace with one another." In his subsequent battles, of which there were several, Muhammad and his followers strictly abided by these conditions, which passed into the *sharia*, along with two others: children, women, and the elderly should not be harmed in war, nor should animals, crops, and buildings.

Two centuries earlier, the North African theologian, Augustine of Hippo, formulated a Christian doctrine of the just war. He argued that Christians should generally use nonviolent methods to resolve conflicts, but that violent aggressors may be resisted by violent means. In particular, Christians may use military force to defend their own communities, to protect the innocent and the weak, and to put right monstrous injustices. Later theologians, such as Thomas Aquinas, added further criteria. Only governments with legitimate authority may wage war, not powerful individuals or groups. War should be a last resort, waged only when every attempt at peaceful settlement has failed. A government authorizing war should acknowledge the extent to which the enemy has justice on its side, and in the event of victory, should uphold the enemy's rights. An attempt should be made to compare the suffering of war with the suffering that war is intended to alleviate, and war should only be waged if the former is likely to be less than the latter. Injury to noncombatants, including soldiers who are injured or have surrendered, should be avoided. Revenge should never be a motive for war, nor should the acquisition of wealth or power. And finally, there should be a reasonable probability of success.

It is highly unlikely that Muhammad had even heard of Augustine of Hippo, let alone been aware of his importance. But, since tribal warfare was a perennial feature of Arab society at that time, it seems likely that he had discussed the ethics of war with Christian acquaintances, including his cousin. And since Augustine's doctrine of the just war had become a familiar part of Christian morality, Muhammad was probably aware of it. So it is hardly surprising that, as a man of the highest moral integrity, he abided by even stricter rules in the conduct of war. Thomas Aquinas and other medieval Christian scholars were probably familiar with Muslim teaching on war; so it is hardly surprising that their criteria for a just war are to a great extent an exposition of the *sharia*. In this way, we may regard Islam and Christianity as carriers of a common tradition concerning warfare.

In addition to their natural revulsion at the acts of Islamic terrorists, most devout Muslims feel disgusted by their hypocrisy. The terrorists claim to be loyal followers of the *sharia*, and at least two terrorist groups include the word *sharia* in their name. Yet even the simplest mind can see that terrorism is an affront to the *sharia;* it involves deceit, and it cannot help but kill and injure children, women, and the elderly. So, although the precise mental state of terrorists is hard to fathom, it is difficult to imagine that their motives for violence are as pure as Muhammad demanded. Some twisted form of pride must surely drive them.

There is comfort and strength in the knowledge that, in opposing terrorism, the West has the *sharia* on its side. A few days after the terrorist attacks on the World Trade Center and the Pentagon, President Bush spoke of a "crusade." To many it seemed an unfortunate word, recalling the medieval wars between Christians and Muslims. But the President was justified in invoking religion. Christians and Muslims have a joint moral heritage that outlaws the killing and maiming of civilians in the conduct of war. And the killing and maiming of civilians, in order to spread fear, is the terrorist's sole aim.

The Legacy

As the centuries and millennia pass, civilizations and cultures rise and decline. Chinese and Indian civilizations glittered for well over a thousand years, but by the medieval period, both were losing their brightness. Greek civilization shone with great intensity for a short period, and then was overtaken by the bolder and less subtle civilization centered on Rome. Two and a half centuries after the fall of Rome, Islamic civilization spread westward across the Roman world, and then eastward to India and beyond. For almost a thousand years, its achievements in almost every sphere of human endeavor were dazzling. For the past two centuries, the culture of western Europe and North America has been in the ascendant, and its achievements have been no less dazzling. And while a dominant people is generally reluctant to acknowledge its debts — indeed, is often unaware of them — each new civilization has borrowed much from earlier civilizations elsewhere.

Yet, the nature of that interrelationship between peoples and cultures is changing rapidly. The Egyptian chemist Geber made significant progress in perfecting the scientific method to its modern form, and the West has used that method to develop, among many other things, technologies for communication that have shrunk the world. Radio and television, and, more recently, e-mail and the Internet, have made the peoples of the world familiar with one another. Thus, knowledge and ideas, which in the past took decades and centuries to cross continents, now take months, days, and minutes. Printing, a technology invented by the Chinese in the ninth century, has in Western hands become vastly more versatile and economical, enabling scholars in every part of the world to share their insights and discoveries. Thus, a kind of global civilization is developing that stands above individual nations and cultures and exerts a growing influence on them.

This global civilization may be regarded as the joint legacy of Islam and the West. And since knowledge, intellectual insights, and ideas comprise the lifeblood of any culture, every culture potentially stands to benefit.

Chapter 3

"What can we do—politically?"
The politics of peace

The Globalization of
Goods and Capital

At the beginning of the nineteenth century, an English economist, David Ricardo, who had earned a small fortune as a banker, put forward a glorious vision of the world economy operating to every nation's advantage and making the entire population of the world richer. He offered clear and precise proofs for all his arguments, which seem incontrovertible. For about a century and a quarter, his vision went virtually unquestioned and guided policy makers throughout the Western world, even justifying the existence of the great empires amassed by Britain, France, Germany, Belgium, and Holland. In the 1930s, in the midst of a global economic slump, another English economist, John Maynard Keynes, cast serious doubt on one half of Ricardo's vision. But by the 1960s, a raft of American economists, led by Milton Friedman, were busily updating Ricardo's theories, and, throughout the 1970s and early 1980s, they won growing support among policy makers. Although few of their senior functionaries are aware of its intellectual pedigree, Ricardian economics infuses the world's two main international economic institutions, the World Trade Organization (WTO) and the International Monetary Fund (IMF). And Ricardo is the invisible guide in government finance and trade departments in America, Europe, and much of the rest of the planet.

The first half of Ricardo's vision is a theory of international trade, known as comparative advantage. For simplicity, he imagined a world economy with two countries, Portugal and England, producing only two goods, cloth and wine. Portugal is better at producing both goods, in that it takes workers fewer hours to produce a cask of wine and a bale of cloth in Portugal than it does in England. So, one might imagine that the Portuguese would produce wine and cloth for themselves and ignore England. But Ricardo pointed out that, if the difference in productivity is greater for one good than the other, it would be better for each country to specialize and trade. Thus, if Portugal has a greater comparative advantage in wine than in cloth, both countries would gain by Portugal producing wine and England producing cloth—and for ships to carry cloth and wine between them.

The implications of this theory, which can be proved by quite a simple piece of mathematics, were, and still are, enormous. In the eighteenth century, trade within Europe was subject to a complex network of tariffs, many of which were more than 25 percent of the value of the goods being traded. The purpose of the tariffs was to protect domestic industries from international competition and to provide revenue for governments. Ricardo's theory showed, to the satisfaction of the British government, that these tariffs made Britain and her trading partners poorer and reduced their rate of economic growth. From the 1820s onward British officials set out to negotiate the mutual abolition of tariffs with her trading partners. If a particular country would not agree, Britain simply abolished its own tariffs on imports from that country. The astonishing success of the British economy soon convinced other European countries that Britain's policy was right, and they too became eager exponents of free trade.

Ricardo's theory also greatly accelerated the expansion of trade with India and the rest of Asia and the Middle East. Britain and the other European powers dismantled the various barriers to trade in the respective empires and spheres of influence. As a consequence, the Asian and Middle Eastern economies became specialists in producing raw materials for European factories, and the factories exported a portion of their output back to Asia and the Middle East. When European explorers penetrated the African interior later in the nineteenth century, the European powers were soon scrambling to impose on its unsuspecting tribespeople the same Ricardian principles.

Above all, Ricardo presided over the astonishing expansion of the American economy, so that by the beginning of the twentieth century President Theodore Roosevelt could envisage the United States competing with, and soon overtaking, the old European nations as a world power. At first, like the Asian economies, North America specialized in producing primary products. But, having the same culture as Europe, it was easily able to emulate European industry. And the growth of American industry gave a further vital twist to the Ricardian scheme. The factories springing up, first on the eastern seaboard and then further west, required massive investment, which Americans at that time could not afford. So, merchant banks and other financial intermediaries sprung up to channel surplus funds from Europe across the Atlantic. Thus, to the globalization of trade was added the globalization of capital.

The second half of Ricardo's vision concerned the link between the supply and demand for goods. He espoused, and then in a novel way explained, a theory first enunciated by a French economist, Jean-Baptiste Say, that supply creates its own demand. This need not be true of a single firm, in that it may produce a good that no one wants, but, according to Ricardo, it is true of the economy as a whole. The main reason is that prices and wages adjust until total demand and supply are in equilibrium. Thus, if total demand is too small to purchase all the goods being produced, prices and wages will fall until demand is sufficient. The main implication is that economies will always tend toward full employment, and unemployed workers will be forced to accept lower wages until they can produce goods cheap enough for people to buy.

Ricardo extended this theory of prices and wages to the international sphere. If an economy is importing more than it is exporting, money will flow out of it in order to pay for the excessive imports. With less money, people will buy fewer goods, both imports and those produced at home. Firms in the home country will then be compelled to reduce prices, and reduce workers' wages; this in turn will make their goods more competitive internationally. Thus, imports will fall, and exports rise, until the two are equal.

The inexorable growth of the European and American economies through the nineteenth and early twentieth

centuries seemed to prove Ricardo's wisdom. No economies in history had enjoyed such expansion over so long
a period, and levels of prosperity were reached that far
surpassed the wildest dreams of past generations. Admit-
tedly, there were occasional economic recessions—when,
for a short period, output and employment would fall—but
a boom soon followed, leading people to conclude that a
capitalist economy was inclined to oscillate. The underlying trend was always upward.

This happy story was interrupted in the period following the First World War, when the capitalist economies entered a major slump from which they could not
rise. Output plummeted and unemployment soared. Governments imposed tariffs in the hope of preserving their
domestic industries, but since every tariff worsened the
problem elsewhere, the net effect was to deepen the slump.
Keynes, an economist whose genius equaled that of Ricardo, pronounced that the second half of Ricardo's vision
was no longer correct, but he vigorously upheld and promoted the first half. He argued that workers, through
their trade unions, were now able to resist reductions in
wages. Firms, faced with falling demand, were unable to
reduce prices, and instead had to reduce output. This, in
turn, forced them to lay off workers, who then had less
money to spend, causing demand, output, and employment to fall even further. In Keynes's view, the Western
economies were caught in this downward spiral, and they
could only be lifted out of it by substantial government
spending.

The New Deal of President Franklin Roosevelt was
the first cautious application of Keynesian economics,
although it was begun shortly before Keynes's major

work was published. In the three decades after the Second World War, all Western governments were committed to spending as much as was necessary to maintain full employment. Keynes himself remained a staunch supporter of free trade, condemning the imposition of trade tariffs as a "beggar-my-neighbor" policy. A global commitment to free trade was enshrined in the General Agreement on Tariffs and Trade, which later became the WTO.

By the 1970s, the power of trade unions in the Western world was starting to diminish. And throughout the 1980s, labor markets changed radically: short and fixed term contracts became common, the typical size of plants and firms fell, and more and more people started their own businesses. As a result, wages and incomes became flexible once more. Now, Keynes's critique lost its force, and Ricardian economics, with a few subtle tweaks, was restored to its full glory. Policy makers could again assure themselves that balanced government budgets and the elimination of trade barriers would be sufficient to enable everyone to become steadily richer. And the IMF, founded in 1944 by a group of economists, led by Keynes, to be a banker to governments, became—and remains—a tireless and dogmatic apostle of Ricardian economics to the countries of Asia, Africa, and Latin America.

False Assumptions

Gandhi, a student of history as well as a great religious teacher and shrewd political leader, observed that India

in the eighteenth century was far more prosperous than
Britain or the rest of Europe. It had a thriving rural economy that produced ample food and the finest cotton and
silk cloth in the world. Its surplus was so great that it
financed the building of fabulous temples and mosques and
supported hosts of artists, writers, and dancers. Small
wonder that British adventurers came to India to make
their fortunes. But, Gandhi said, free trade had ruined
the Indian economy. By the end of the nineteenth century,
India's cloth production had almost disappeared, it often
could not feed itself, and its people spent much of their
time in miserable idleness. Through the economic process
analyzed by Ricardo, India had come to specialize in the
growing of raw cotton and silk, while Britain specialized
in spinning and weaving. But India's former spinners and
weavers were unable to find alternative work, and since
so much of India's land was now turned over to the supply of Britain's cotton mills, food was perennially scarce.
Far from making India richer, free trade had simply made
Britain richer at India's expense. The spinning wheel for
Gandhi was the symbol of Indian independence. In his
view, independence was not merely a change of government, but a withdrawal from the global system of trade
and a return to self-reliance.

While the details differ in each case, Gandhi's theory
of impoverishment through trade can be applied to most
countries of Asia and Africa. A few Middle Eastern countries have been partially spared from poverty by the dis-
covery of oil, but wealth from oil merely masks the underlying economic devastation, which will be exposed as
soon as oil runs out or demand for it falls. Gandhi himself
never grappled with Ricardo's economic theory. If he had

done so, he would quickly have seen that, while the theory's logic itself is impeccable, its crucial underlying assumption is false. The theory of comparative advantage assumes that people can move quickly and easily from one occupation to another. In his hypothetical example, spinners and weavers in Portugal learn the skills to make wine, while the workers in English vineyards learn how to use spinning wheels and looms. In nineteenth-century India, faced with cloth spun and woven in British factories, the rural spinners and weavers were, according to Ricardian theory, required to find work growing cotton and breeding silk worms. Unfortunately, workers frequently cannot acquire new skills, nor move to the places where these skills may need to be practiced. And when they fail to adapt and move, they become idle and impoverished. In India this situation was made even worse by the fact that the expansion of cotton growing and silk farming required little additional labor. Instead, farms hitherto producing crops for local consumption simply shifted to cotton and silk.

At this point, the second half of Ricardo's vision should apply: unemployed workers reduce their wage demands until they become cheap enough to employ. But if people are already living near the level of subsistence, there is little scope for wage reductions, and if there are few firms in existence with scope for expansion, even starvation wages will not help. Thus, instead of Ricardo's smooth return to full employment, there is Keynes's vicious downward spiral of falling demand and falling employment, causing demand and employment to fall even further. This was precisely what occurred in India throughout the nineteenth century, and continued into the twentieth. And it is the cruel dilemma that now faces much of the Middle East, large chunks of the rest of Asia, almost the whole of Africa, and most of Latin America.

But why can these poor countries not follow the American example of the nineteenth century, attracting capital from abroad? This is the prescription advocated by the IMF and the other current exponents of global capitalism. Indeed, they argue that, in an age of transnational corporations and sophisticated financial money markets, it should be relatively easy to lure foreign investors, eager to take advantage of low wages. And the experience of South Korea, Malaysia, and Thailand, the so-called Asian tigers in the 1970s and 1980s, seems to confirm this optimism. But when, in the past fifteen years, governments have taken every drop of the IMF medicine, the economic cure has still not occurred. The reason is quite simple and obvious: modern manufacturing industry is now so mechanized, requiring a few skilled workers rather than armies of unskilled workers, that low wages make little difference to costs. It is far more important to be near the affluent markets of the West, so that designs can be altered rapidly in response to changing tastes and fashions and the time taken to deliver the finished goods can be minimized. The small pockets of recent economic success in poor countries, such as Bangalore in South India, have depended on an existing pool of highly skilled workers able to speak fluent English. And these workers are engaged not on production lines in factories, but in research and software production.

Yet even when poor countries succeed in attracting Western capital, experience shows it to be a mixed blessing. In the short run it provides jobs and incomes. But, whereas in America in the nineteenth century, Americans themselves ran the new industries, today in Asia and Africa, transnational corporations send their own managers and technicians to supervise their factories. Thus, the transfer of skill and expertise is limited, and, worse still, the sense of inferiority to the West is deepened. Then, if local wages rise significantly or if changing global conditions induce changes in strategy, transnational corporations are free to dismantle their factories and move elsewhere, leaving the local people worse off than before.

It has been repeated so often in recent times that the rich in the world are getting richer and the poor are getting poorer that we have almost come to regard this as an immutable economic law—equivalent to a natural law, such as night following day. Yet while the passing of night and day has a tranquil and unchanging rhythm, worsening inequality has a beat that grows louder and faster. As the plight of the poor becomes more desperate, they become more willing to resort to desperate measures. Visitors to the West Bank and Gaza, witnessing the appalling conditions in which most Palestinians live, are no longer surprised at the flow of young men volunteering to be suicide bombers. And these Palestinian enclaves are positively luxurious compared with the destitution suffered by many hundreds of millions elsewhere across the Muslim world and beyond. If these destitute millions were unaware of Western affluence, their resentment and anger, like that of Job in the Bible, might be directed against God. But most see pictures of the West on communal television sets or hear on communal radio sets of Western economic and political involvement in their countries; and many see Western aid workers in expensive vehicles. So, the West's relationship with them seems, in the stark image coined by Tolstoy, like a big fat man riding on the back of a small thin man, the big man occasionally reaching forward to put a morsel of food in the small man's mouth. And Islamic terrorism seems like the small man biting the tip of the big man's finger.

The Globalization of People and Expertise

Until about two centuries ago, trade between continents was minimal, confined to a few luxuries such as jewelry, fine silks, and spices. Even between neighboring countries, trade involved only a negligible portion of total output. Yet, the movement of people has always been huge. As far as scientists can tell, *homo sapiens* evolved in eastern Africa and spread from there across the globe. And archeologists and historians tell us of many more recent migrations. For example, four millennia ago, hundreds of thousands of Aryans moved from the central Asian steppes into India and Europe, and a later western movement from central Asia led ultimately to the fall of Rome. A millennium and a half ago, Angles and Saxons spread from their German heartlands across the North Sea to Britain; then Vikings moved southward from Scandinavia into Ireland, Britain, and France. At the same time, large groups from Iran and Syria were sailing to the Malabar coast of India. And since the sixteenth century, emigrants from Europe have settled in vast numbers over three entire continents, Australasia, North and South America, largely displacing the existing inhabitants. These movements of population have often provoked violence—readers of the Bible are familiar with the battles between the immigrant Hebrews and the native Canaanites. But through a varying mixture of slaughter, intermarriage, and territorial division, peace has in most cases been established.

As people have migrated, they have carried their skills and expertise across the world and also learned skills from the people among whom they settle. By about two millennia ago, men and women throughout the Eurasian landmass had acquired the knowledge to forge metal tools and to fire and glaze clay pots. The art of cooking, which made food more digestible and thus led to great improvements in human health and strength, seems to have spread from China. And the most important skill of all, breeding large grains from small grass seeds, seems to have developed in the fertile crescent between the rivers Tigris and Euphrates. This marked the birth of agriculture, enabling food to be produced far more plentifully. Agricultural skills were taken across the world with remarkable speed, so the human population multiplied. The final victory of settled farming over nomadic herding occurred in the American Wild West—a victory both celebrated and lamented in numerous Hollywood movies depicting the conflicts between homesteaders and ranchers.

Yet, in the recent past, through a mixture of political action and entrepreneurial energy, the nature of globalization has been turned on its head. Whereas goods and capital were once virtually static, now they hurtle across the planet; and whereas people and skills once moved across the planet, now they are forced to be static. Western governments have taken pride in lifting all controls on trade and investment, but they have imposed ever harsher measures against immigration. And just as the globalization of goods and capital has impoverished many countries in Asia and Africa, so the suppression of global movements of people has locked the populations of those countries in their poverty. This reverse globalization is assumed, and implicitly advocated, by Ricardo's theory of comparative advantage. In his hypothetical example, the English would gain most by migrating to Portugal, where they could become more efficient in both cloth and wine production. But since Ricardo disallows international migration, workers are compelled to endure the low efficiency of their homeland.

In the modern world, the uncontrolled migration of the past is no longer feasible. There can be little doubt that, if Western nations lifted all controls, there would be a flood of immigrants from Africa, Asia, and Latin America. And while the battles between Hebrews and Canaanites would not be reenacted on the streets of Memphis, Manchester, and Munich, there would be other and more intractable problems. Western governments are now committed to provide health care and education to the poor along with direct cash payments. Thus, massive immigration would put an intolerable strain on government finances. There is a land shortage in parts of many Western countries, and a rapid rise in population would greatly worsen congestion. While the gradual mixing of cultures has many beneficial effects, as America's long experience shows, massive and sudden immigration would lead to civil strife. And, of course, there is the danger that, hidden among the law-abiding immigrants, there would be gangs of terrorists and criminals.

Nonetheless, a controlled flow of immigrants from the poorer to the richer nations, who stay for a period of years before returning home, offers profound benefits to both sides. Asians, Africans, and Latin Americans who have lived, received some higher education, and worked in North America and Europe generally become sympathetic to Western civilization. Their former suspicion and even hostility, based largely on ignorance, is usually replaced by respect and admiration—albeit tempered by some justified degree of criticism. When they go back to their native countries, they apply many of the ideas and values that they learned in the West. And since they tend to occupy influential positions, they become a strong force for good relations with the West. Indeed, one of the lasting legacies of the British empire is the degree to which the populations, especially the elites, in the former colonies have imbibed Western values, and remained pro-Western in their attitudes. It is significant that, among Muslim countries, Pakistan, which was under British rule for almost two centuries, has been most consistently supportive toward America and the West. Thus, if Western countries welcomed more— many more—young men and women from poorer countries, enabling them to stay for five or ten years, the world would gradually become more friendly and less threatening—and also more willing to accept Western investment.

The benefits to the poorer countries themselves would be even greater. The huge economic success of America over the last century and half was built on the spirit of adventure, which both makes people willing to travel the world in pursuit of economic betterment and willing to start new businesses. American immigration and American capitalism are closely connected. Similarly, young people from

poor nations who have traveled to the West, for education and for practical experience, return home as budding
capitalists, eager to put their Western skills to profitable
use. Giving young people from poorer nations direct
experience of the West is by far the most effective form of
assistance to those nations—much better than direct aid,
which is liable merely to engender a spirit of dependency.

However, the ability of Asians and Africans to start
businesses at home depends to a great extent on curbing
the globalization of goods. Three and a half centuries ago,
a wise political economist named William Petty advocated
the use of tariffs to protect "infant industries" from foreign competition. Without tariffs, he said, new enterprises
might be drowned by cheap imports before they could
become established. In the post-war period, with Western approval, Japan erected a tariff wall behind which its
devastated economy could recover; a little later the Asian
tigers all erected similar trade barriers to encourage domestic industry. But a tariff wall need not be temporary, to be
pulled down as soon as local firms can compete in world
markets. Ricardian economics rightly predicts that, as soon
as tariffs disappear, firms without comparative advantage
will be destroyed. Rather a country, or group of neighboring countries, could have a permanent tariff wall, behind
which they allow a multiplicity of different industries to
develop, meeting the great bulk of local needs. Indeed, to
see the success of such a policy, one need look no further
than the European Union (EU), which in essence is a
customs union, with no internal barriers to trade, and a
common external barrier. Since its inception in 1957, the
member countries have become largely self-reliant and
now enjoy a remarkable degree of both prosperity and

stability. The EU is, of course, guilty of monstrous hypocrisy, since it strongly supports the WTO in its efforts to break down trade barriers elsewhere in the world. Countries in Asia and Africa would be wise to defy the WTO and follow the EU's example.

In the context of trade controls, the free movement of capital across the globe is liable to lose its malign effects and become benign. Local companies in the poorer nations, set up by Western-trained entrepreneurs, would be able to attract capital from the West because they would have secure access to their home market. At the same time, transnational companies would now be able to earn profits in the poorer nations by setting up permanent plants that would make goods for the local market. Thus, they would transfer both their technology and their skills to the poorer countries. Again, the EU provides many examples of this process. Japanese and other Asian companies, finding themselves prevented by European trade restrictions from exporting successfully to Europe, have instead set up factories within Europe itself, and management techniques pioneered by Japanese firms have spread rapidly throughout European industry.

Politics after September 11

The most vibrant city in the world, the city that never sleeps, became not only somber and achingly sad in the aftermath of September 11, but also astonishingly gentle and generous. Car horns fell silent, truck and cab drivers no longer shouted abuse, young people escorted older people across the street, and criminals restrained their larcenous instincts. Those who had lived in London through the blitz of 1940, and survived, were not surprised. When the people of a city or town suffer a collective tragedy, they draw together in mutual concern and support. And wartime London and New York share another, more subtle, moral attitude: stoic defiance, which excludes any desire for revenge. Londoners refused to be cowed, and yet had little hatred of the Germans raining down bombs; New Yorkers also remain unbowed, and also are surprisingly free of loathing for their cruel enemies. When Winston Churchill strode over the rubble in his boiler suit, he expressed this spirit in words of eloquent simplicity: "London can take it." Mayor Giuliani expressed the same spirit in his calm resilience and honest dignity.

But, though the mood of London and New York are the same, the wider political context is wholly different. Londoners, and their fellow Brits, had a clear enemy, the Nazi regime led by Hitler, and they knew that Nazism had to be defeated by creating a more powerful army, navy, and air force than Hitler possessed. They also knew that once Nazism was defeated, they needed to make friends with Germany and together build a peaceful Europe. New Yorkers, and their fellow Americans, have no clear enemy, since Islamic terrorism is hidden and elusive. Indeed, New York financiers are grimly aware that terrorists may be working in their midst. Only insiders could have successfully traded in those gold, oil, and share futures. And they know that a war against terrorism can have no victorious conclusion, after which the hand of friendship can be extended. When one part of the terrorist network has been defeated, other parts will remain a threat.

This dilemma, which is simultaneously moral and practical, confronts the whole of the Western world, and even the whole of humanity. And it is equally difficult for those wanting to wage war and those wanting to make peace. If there can be no military victory, there can also be no treaty or settlement that ends hostility. In conventional negotiations between rival powers, each side presents demands, and then each side offers concessions, until finally an agreement is reached that is acceptable to both. But the Islamic terrorists are willing to offer no concessions, because for them the enemy is Western civilization itself, with its baleful domination of Muslim civilization. So, while force of arms cannot defeat them, even the most generous diplomacy cannot appease them. The old political division between hawks and doves, warmongers and peacemakers, no longer applies.

Many people already understand this, and even though political rhetoric and action mainly continue to follow the old tunes and rhythms, a different melody is already audible in the background. It has suddenly become possible to question the virtue of global capitalism without being regarded as a dangerous subversive or laughable crank. It is gradually becoming possible to suggest a more open and welcoming attitude to migration, without being dismissed as a utopian dreamer. Conventional assumptions are crumbling, and the political and economic values built upon them are showing cracks. As we speculate about terrorists acquiring nuclear devices and biological and chemical weapons, we know that a new way of ordering the world is urgently needed.

Other global issues are also being looked at afresh, most notably environmental pollution, which is ultimately an even greater threat to humanity than terrorism. Western governments have always been half-hearted about global warming, because they fear that any serious attempt to combat it could throw sand in the engine of global capitalism. But, since terrorism has now thrown whole rocks into that engine, this timidity now seems petty and absurd. The political impetus required to limit the globalization of goods and capital, and to allow the globalization of people and expertise, is the same kind of impetus required to regulate the emissions of greenhouse gases. There is no shortage of practical ideas as to how this may be done, from direct controls to tradable permits. Moreover, once the people of individual countries become economically self-reliant, they will have a direct interest in conserving their resources.

Before September 11, the Western economies led by America were already sliding toward recession. The terrorist atrocities only accelerated that slide. Some European economies, most notably that of Germany, also slipped into recession. Past experience suggests that, in a year or two, the American and German economies will bounce back. But Japan provides a dark warning that mature capitalist economies need not always prove resilient. For the past decade, the Japanese economy has stagnated, and although the Japanese government has applied all the conventional remedies advocated by Keynes, hugely boosting public expenditure and slashing interest rates to zero, the economy refuses to revive. It seems that consumers are broadly content with the material standard they have already attained and simply save any additional income. At one point, in a desperate attempt to boost consumption, the government issued vouchers to be exchanged in shops for goods, but most Japanese merely cut expenditure of their own money by the equivalent amount.

In spiritual terms the Japanese attitude to consumption is commendable. Jesus and the Buddha, along with most other religious leaders over the centuries, have advocated material simplicity. And in a world where billions are abjectly poor, the rampant consumerism of the West seems immoral. Yet, in a capitalist system, demand for goods and services is the engine that drives the economic motor. If the engine splutters, not only do the rich become less rich, but the poor become even poorer.

International agreements to control trade offer a resolution to this paradox, boosting economic activity to the benefit of all. And if they were combined with antipollution controls, and also a temporary cessation of migration from poor to rich countries, the economies of the world could enjoy a new kind of boom that steadily reduced inequality, and thus could be sustained. To begin to imagine such a boom, one may consider a single, vital industry, the production of automobiles. Suppose the governments of the world agreed that, over the coming twenty-five years, the use of fossil fuels in automobiles would be phased out; at the same time, tariffs on the international trade of automobiles would be gradually raised. Immediately, automobile companies would recruit armies of researchers to develop new kinds of engines, and they would then build new factories to produce these engines. Moreover, these factories would have to be located in every part of the world, in order to avoid the tariffs. If these engines were more expensive to run, public transport would become more competitive, and so would expand. And the countries of the Middle East currently dependent on oil— whose rulers have frittered most of the oil revenues away on lavish social provision for their people and obscene luxury for themselves—would have a compelling incentive to invest their remaining revenues in creating new industries to provide goods and jobs in the future.

If such a scenario seems a little fanciful, one may take a dose of new realism from the IMF's latest *World Economic Outlook*, published in late September, though written prior to September 11. It concludes there is no "significant relationship . . . between capital liberalization and growth," adding that "it would be a mistake for [poor] countries to think that involvement with global capital markets offers a magic, near-term fix for their problems." When the IMF is having severe doubts about Ricardian economics—even before the catastrophe of September 11—then the rest of us can safely assume that the Ricardian era is quickly passing.

Toward Political Freedom

In the mid-eighteenth century, the French philosopher Jean-Jacques Rousseau famously began his treatise *The Social Contract* with the words, "Man was born free, and he is everywhere in chains." He then grappled with the relationship between individual and collective freedom within society. He recognized that individuals have certain economic freedoms, such as what goods to buy, what work to do, and how to invest their wealth. But these freedoms are exercised within a framework of laws that constrain and limit them. France in Rousseau's time was ruled by a monarchy with the power to impose laws, which Rousseau loathed, and he wondered how the making of laws could itself become free. His answer lay in the concept of the general will, in which individuals freely align their own wills with that of the community as a whole, expressed through voting. He proposed that the people should initially elect a parliament whose members draft laws. These laws should then be accepted or rejected by the people in a direct ballot. When a particular law was proposed, some would be likely to be in favor of it, and some against it, and vigorous debate should occur. But as soon as a vote is taken, everyone should willingly submit to the will of the majority.

Among the nations of the West, only Switzerland follows Rousseau's idea of the people voting on laws—although some states in America, such as California, have frequent referenda on various issues. In every other country, the elected representatives both draft and pass laws. And all Western nations allow people to continue to express disapproval of laws even after they have come into force. In short, the principle of the general will, in which laws enacted by democratic means are binding on everyone, has been adopted throughout the West and is the foundation of every Western political constitution.

Islam, as we have seen, began to grapple with the relationship between individual and collective freedom twelve centuries earlier. Muhammad himself expressed the principle of the general will in his much-quoted saying, "My community will never agree on an error." At that time, no system of popular voting had ever existed in any large country or empire; the system of democracy in ancient Athens, in which every male citizen attended the political gatherings, could only work in a single small city or town. Besides, even if the Muslim legal scholars had considered popular voting, they would quickly have dismissed it as impractical. The Arab empire was too large, communication was too slow and unreliable, and too many people were nomadic. So, they put their trust in judges, who were required to be sensitive to popular opinion. Yet there is nothing in the *sharia* itself requiring that judges be the medium of the general will. And in the present age, when communication is quick and reliable and almost everyone is settled, popular voting is surely a preferable medium. Indeed it is hard to imagine that the great al-Shafii would not have been delighted with modern forms of democracy.

It is tempting to say that the system of government is a matter for each country to determine for itself. In this light, the fact that many Middle Eastern countries are highly autocratic, with rulers who habitually ignore popular opinion, should not concern anyone outside those countries themselves. This isolationist argument would perhaps be valid if populations were entirely static. But today most Western nations have substantial numbers of Muslims, most of whose families originate in the Middle East. It is important that they should feel that the system of government under which they live, and to which they must submit, is compatible with their religion. And if we are to negotiate greater freedom of movement between nations, then it becomes vital that some common political principles, which all reasonable people can accept, are agreed upon.

The atrocity of September 11 has been widely, and rightly, interpreted as an attack on democracy. In a democracy, dissent is expressed in open debate and through voting. So, any kind of intimidation, by which tiny majorities try to assert themselves over the general will, is a dagger aimed at democracy's heart. It follows that the war against terrorism is in defense of democracy. Yet the conduct of this war involves a profound moral and political contradiction. It can only be seriously waged with the cooperation of highly undemocratic governments in the Middle East, and in the face of autocracy, terrorism is, in many people's eyes, a valid form of resistance. Indeed, the West has a long, and often honorable, tradition of supporting terrorism in the name of freedom. Many westerners supported the terrorist campaign conducted by the African National Congress (ANC) against the apartheid regime of South Africa, and, when the ANC's leader, Nelson Mandela, who had been imprisoned for terrorist activities, was elected president of South Africa, the whole world applauded. Going further back, the fighters in the French Resistance fought the Nazi occupation of their country by means of terrorism, which was the only strategy at their disposal. They are lauded as heroes. And in the 1980s the American and British governments gave financial and military support to the *mujahideen* (holy warriors), who included Osama bin Laden, in their guerilla war against the Soviet-backed regime in Kabul. British commandoes even instructed them in terrorism's dark arts.

In the heat of crisis, one enemy's enemies quickly becomes one's friend. So, several autocratic Middle Eastern regimes, which are themselves threatened by Islamic militants, have been welcomed as supporters in the war against terrorism. But as American leaders never tire of repeating, this war will not be over in five days, five months, or even five years; it is a long, long war. And a vital element in ultimate victory is that all the peoples of the Middle East and beyond must enjoy political freedom. Only then does terrorism lose its moral and persuasive force. As the multiplicity of constitutional arrangements in the West demonstrates, there is no single form that freedom must take. In every country of the world the cultural traditions and the ethnic mix are different, with differing political implications. But by one means or another, the principle of the general will, enunciated by Muhammad and Rousseau, must be enacted.

Thus the war against terrorism is not ultimately a matter of military incursions and protective action. It is a matter of diplomacy and negotiation, argument and discussion. Of course, autocratic regimes will resist change. But, even if they care nothing for freedom, all autocrats want their countries to prosper, if only to allay popular discontent, and they look with dismay and fear at the poverty in which most of their people live. This gives power to the forces of freedom. By proposing to turn globalization on its head, replacing the globalization of goods and capital with the globalization of people and knowledge, the West would offer a route to prosperity — and to dignity. And this new form of globalization depends on the spread of freedom.

On the path to freedom, the conflict between the Israelis and Palestinians is the largest boulder. How, the leaders and the people alike of the Middle East ask, can the

West be sincere in its espousal of freedom when it supports the Israeli oppression of the Palestinian Arabs? Even the most generous proposals ever offered by the Israelis go only a short way toward satisfying Palestinian demands. But if this conflict is utterly intractable in the present political order, it begins to become soluble in the new political order of universal freedom. And the founding father of Zionism, Theodor Herzl, would heartily approve the new order. He wanted a united Palestine, in which Jew and Muslim were equal and free under the law, and he understood that such a political order conformed to the best traditions of Judaism and Islam alike. Modern Israelis would understandably view with skepticism any return to the original Zionist vision. All the Arab states around them are autocratic, and they would distrust the commitment of Palestinian Arabs to democracy. But if the whole of the Middle East were moving toward democracy, the picture would be transformed. Thus a permanent resolution of the Israeli-Palestinian conflict is both a crucial means of achieving the new political order and a priceless prize of its achievement.

Chapter 4

"What can we do—religiously?"
The religion of peace

The Globalization of
Creeds and Sects

The sayings of Jesus, recorded in the gospels of Matthew, Mark, and Luke, reveal him as a man of immense wisdom and wit. He expressed profound moral and spiritual ideas with wonderful simplicity and precision, and he encapsulated these ideas in stories and metaphors that grip the imagination. His actions reveal him as a man of immense compassion and generosity. He sought to help all those in need, regardless of race, class, or religion. Like the thousands of people who came to listen to him, we feel drawn toward him and want to follow his teachings. Yet there was nothing original in what he said. Every idea in every saying can be found elsewhere in the words of earlier teachers. Moreover, he made no claim to originality. Indeed, he made no claim whatever about himself, except that he was inspired by God. He believed he was articulating in fresh form the ancient faith of Abraham. And he referred to himself, according to these three gospels, as "the son of man," the same epithet that the prophet Ezekiel had used about himself. Like Ezekiel, he saw himself standing in a long tradition of teachers who articulate to the people of their time universal and unchanging truths.

Paul of Tarsus, the first major figure to carry the message of Jesus beyond the region where Jesus himself traveled, probably never heard Jesus speak. In his letters he rarely refers to the words of Jesus. He took for granted that Jesus was echoing the teachings of earlier Jewish prophets, whose words he had learned in childhood. Besides, as he wrote in his letter to the Romans (2.15), the divine truths expressed by every great teacher are "written on all men's hearts." Paul, however, saw in the story of Jesus, in particular his death and resurrection, the perfect expression of these truths. As he wrote to the Romans (6.4): "We are buried with Christ, so that as he was raised from the dead by the glory of the Father, we too might walk in newness of life." Paul saw people as addicted—chained—to moral and spiritual evil, which oppressed and destroyed them. By identifying with the death of Christ, they could be saved from this addiction and set free.

John, who almost undoubtedly wrote his gospel some years after Paul's hectic endeavors, took a somewhat different approach to the figure of Jesus. John was steeped in the philosophy of the Greek Stoics, which had passed into Jewish thought through Philo, a member of the large Jewish community in Alexandria. John took from Philo the concept of *Logos*, usually translated as "Word," which signifies divine energy present throughout the world and the universe, and which creates and sustains every object and living being. A similar concept, referred to as "wis-

dom," appears in the later writings of the Jewish Bible (the
Old Testament, as Christians call it): Wisdom, according to
the Book of Proverbs, was God's agent in the process of
creation, and continues to dwell in human minds. According to John, Jesus Christ was *Logos* made flesh: he was
in perfect union with the Word, and thence completely free
from the bonds of evil. And ordinary men and women
could share this union with the Word by unifying their
lives with the life of Jesus.

Both Paul and John, in their distinct ways, were
making a higher claim for Jesus than Jesus appears to
have made for himself. And without doubt, they regarded
becoming a disciple of Jesus Christ as the highest form of
religion available for humankind. But neither of their philosophies denied the potential validity of other religions;
on the contrary, their philosophies were open and inclu-
sive. Since, according to Paul, the divine truth is written
on all human hearts, and since, according to John, the
divine Word is present everywhere, we should expect
other religions to overlap greatly with the religion of Christ.
John's gospel goes even further: it contains the promise
that the divine spirit will lead people toward the fullness
of truth (16.13) —implying that the followers of Christ
remain seekers, like the followers of other teachers, with
only partial understanding. Even the apparent claim of
uniqueness, that "no one comes to the Father but by me,"
(14.6) is properly understood in its context as the oppo-
site: it is through discerning the Word, present in every
person and throughout creation, that we reach God.

The respective philosophies of John and Paul, however, laid the foundation for a grand theological edifice
that excluded all other religions. John's reflections on *Logos*

led to an intense debate on God's relationship with Jesus. The general thrust of the debate was to show that God's presence within Jesus was entirely different from his presence in other people. Some theologians even suggested that Jesus' body was illusory and that he was wholly divine. Eventually, in the fifth century, a formula was agreed by most Christian leaders stating that Jesus uniquely had two natures, one divine and one human, existing in perfect unity; and hence, through Jesus, and Jesus alone, human beings have access to God. Paul's reflections on the crucifixion led to the notion that all human beings were inherently sinful and that the death of this God-man was a complete and perfect sacrifice for their sin, enabling them to escape the divine punishment that they deserved. Therefore, if people believe in Christ as divine, and accept that he died for them, they can be eternally reconciled with God.

Once this edifice was complete, Christianity was committed to bringing the whole of humanity under its roof. If people were condemned to eternal alienation from God outside Christianity, then Christians had an urgent and compelling duty to bring them in. Thus, Christianity became the first religion to have truly global ambitions.

Islam was the second religion with global ambitions. Muhammad, like Jesus, made quite modest claims about himself. He saw himself as a channel—a prophet—through which God was speaking to a particular people at a particular time. But even for the Arab people at the turn of the sixth and seventh centuries, the message was not new. Rather, it was, according to Muhammad, a fresh expression of the ancient faith that they had received from Abraham. Moreover, several verses in the Koran—the book of the words that Muhammad believed he had received from God—indicate that God appoints individuals as prophets in every age and for every nation. Thus the Koran recognizes the authority of Jesus, as well as that of the ancient prophets of Judaism.

Just as Jesus himself concentrated his attention on his Jewish compatriots, so Muhammad was concerned solely with the tribes of the Arabian peninsula. But since the Arabs began their campaign of conquest soon after Muhammad's death, the task of turning his faith into a global religion was urgent. As Muhammad had been so clear about the nature of his relationship with God, this was quite simple: they declared that the Koran was the final and complete message from God, valid for all time and in all places.

False Assumptions

At the start of the fifth century the famous theologian and bishop Augustine of Hippo authorized the first specifically religious war that history records. The enemy was a group of Christians in North Africa known as Donatists, after their founder Donatus. They wanted the church to consist only of those who were spiritually and morally pure and refused to accept baptism and communion from ministers who were in any way tainted. They also seem to have asserted that a pure Christian has immediate access to God's Spirit, and hence has direct knowledge of the truth. Augustine saw clearly that, in striving for perfection within Christianity, the Donatists threatened to destroy it. In the first place, the church as an organization could never guarantee the purity of its ministers. Any requirement for absolute purity would lead to perpetual disputes, as people found fault with particular ministers. More fundamentally, however, if people have direct access to God, then they have no need for Jesus Christ as the mediator between God and humanity and no need for his sacrificial death. Augustine, therefore, thus pronounced that the Donatists must be suppressed by force.

Over the next thirteen centuries, Christendom continued to stamp out heresy by means of physical suppression, sometimes involving great brutality. And the common feature of almost all heresies was that, implicitly or explicitly, they undermined Christianity's claim to have a monopoly of truth. (Indeed, the word "heresy" derives from a Greek word meaning "freedom of choice.") Some heresies, like that promoted by Arius, denied the divinity of Jesus Christ; some, like that promoted by Abelard, denied that the crucifixion was a sacrifice for sin, seeing it simply as a supreme example of love; some, like that of Pelagius, asserted that salvation was purely a matter of making good moral choices, so there would be no need for theological doctrines; and many, like that of Donatus, asserted the ability of all Christians to communicate directly with God.

The most bitter of all conflicts within Christianity was that between Catholics and Protestants, and when this was combined with competing nationalisms, as in the Thirty Years' War of the early seventeenth century, it led to the most terrible bloodshed. This conflict was not between a rigid set of doctrines and spiritual freedom, but between two rival sets of doctrines. The differences between Catholic and Protestant theology has many dimensions, and

Protestantism itself has many variations. But in essence, the dispute was over the source of doctrinal authority, with Protestants believing the New Testament to be the only source and Catholics asserting that the church as an organization had divine authority to interpret the New Testament.

Islam has its own similar record of internal dissent and conflict. By the early eighth century, less than a hundred years after Muhammad's death, an eminent scholar, Hasan al-Basr, was criticizing the greed and hypocrisy of the senior clergy, who took pleasure in telling the people how to behave and what to believe, but who themselves were utterly unscrupulous and materialistic. A few decades later, the Sufi movement began. The first known Sufi was a woman named Rabia, who went to live in the desert and devoted herself to attaining mystical union with God. People soon flocked to see her, sensing spiritual warmth within her that was absent from the clergy, whom she openly criticized for using the fear of hell as a means of enforcing their authority. By the time Rabia died in 801, there were hundreds of Sufi mystics, some living in solitude, and others traveling from place to place, teaching all who would listen. Their message was similar to that of the Donatists: every individual can receive direct guidance and comfort from God. Most Sufis concluded that the clergy, who interpreted and expounded the Koran, were actually barriers to true religion. Instead, they said, we need spiritual guides who can show us how to open our souls to the divine spirit. Some Sufis, such as Hallaj, went even further. He taught that God dwells within every person, so all people can be prophets. To emphasize his conviction, he frequently declared, "I am the Truth." The

Muslim clergy rightly perceived that Hallaj, who attracted a large following, was undermining the unique position of the Koran, and they arrested and crucified him.

Despite frequent efforts to suppress it, the Sufi movement has continued to this day. It was mainly Sufis who carried Islam—their mystical version of it—to West Africa, India, and Southeast Asia. However, the deepest division within Islam, that between Sunni and Shia, occurred late in the eighth century. As with Protestantism and Catholicism within Christianity, the two represent rival views of authority. The Sunni, who have always formed the majority, assert that the Koran is the ultimate source of authority, while the Shia place their trust in the divinely inspired interpretations of their human leaders. Beyond this lies a further division on their view of history: the Sunni believe that the ultimate destiny of Islam is to rule the world, whereas the Shia regard Muslims as a righteous minority awaiting the coming of a messianic figure—the *Mahdi*—who will usher in a society of perfect justice. Like Catholics and Protestants, Sunni and Shia have a long history of mutual persecution. Recent examples are the ruthless slaughter by the Taliban and Saddam Hussein of the Shia minorities in their respective countries and the oppression by the Iranian regime of its Sunni minority.

Over and above the conflicts within Christianity and Islam, there is, as we have seen, the long history of conflicts between them. The triumph of orthodoxy over heresy in both religions makes rivalry between them inevitable. Christian orthodoxy, in both its Catholic and Protestant forms, must condemn Islam, along with all other religions, as, at best, defective and, at worst, downright evil. Likewise Islamic orthodoxy, in both its Sunni and Shia forms, must make the same condemnation of Christianity. Of course, rival religions need not be deadly enemies, and happily, there are many instances, both in the past and in the present, where the competition between Christianity and Islam has been peaceful. But, since human nature is aggressive, violence is an ever-present danger. Islamic militancy of the kind pursued by al Qaeda is simply its latest manifestation.

This conflict and rivalry begs a question that is rarely asked: Why in both religions has orthodoxy appeared triumphant over heresy? If, in Christianity, Arians and Pelagians had won the day, and within Islam, Sufism had come to dominate, the two religions could happily coexist, with people drawing freely from the wisdom of both. The answer is simple, and yet carries huge implications: orthodoxy requires large and cohesive religious organizations; heretics, by contrast, are interested only in small, loose-knit communities. Since Christianity and Islam in their orthodox forms want to conquer every heart and mind, they need global spiritual armies, and these spiritual armies, like military armies, must of necessity suppress disobedience and dissent within their own ranks. Heretics only desire companions to accompany them on their spiritual journey. Thus, the major religious organizations will always tend to be orthodox.

But the triumph of orthodoxy over heresy has always been more apparent than real. The history of heresy in both Christianity and Islam is punctuated by figures of hugely popular appeal, whose teachings have satisfied the spiritual yearnings of ordinary men and women. We cannot, of course, know precisely what the mass of people believed hundreds of years ago. But the persistent appeal of heresy suggests at the very least that the doctrinal formulae of Christian and Islamic orthodoxy have always had many doubters, and, quite possibly, never commanded the assent of the majorities in the lands where they were promulgated. And today in the West, heresy may be winning. Opinion polls on religious belief consistently show that many people regard Jesus simply as a great and wise teacher, and they see the role of Jesus, and other such teachers, as showing people how to lead good lives. Hence, they reject both the notion of Jesus as a unique God-man and the idea of his death as a sacrifice that saves them from inherent sin. In short, the religion of the West is predominantly Arian and Pelagian.

Behind the rejection of orthodoxy lies the rejection of the assumption on which orthodoxy, Christian and Islamic alike, is based: there is some ultimate truth, or set of truths, capable of being defined and articulated.

The Globalization of Wisdom and Symbols

In past eras, when science had not yet discovered the complexity, enormity, and antiquity of the universe, it seemed quite possible that the human mind could formulate some overarching philosophical and theological theory about existence. And when Islam and Christianity mostly occupied different parts of the globe, and when communication between them was intermittent and slow, it was relatively easy for their leaders to claim that their particular

theory was beyond question. Yet in most Western countries today, members of different religious groups live
side by side, and books and electronic media constantly
remind us of the multiplicity of religious beliefs and practices. It seems inherently unlikely that one religion is
right, while all the others are wrong. Moreover, we are
now aware that our species is one of hundreds of thousands, our planet is one of millions, and that the universe
is billions of years old. Aware of these facts, we are compelled to admit that our minds can only comprehend a
tiny fraction of existence. Hence, the dogmas of orthodox
Christianity and Islam have quite simply been rendered
absurd. Indeed, acceptance of religious dogma of any kind
involves intellectual dishonesty.

It is tempting, therefore, to dismiss religion as outdated.
And, in the light of the bloodshed caused by religious doctrines, it is doubly tempting to oppose the very existence
of religion. The outrage of September 11 is merely the latest
vile crime against humanity conducted in the name of some
human conception of God. Surely, therefore, it is time to
destroy the sources of all conceptions of God. Yet human
beings seem innately religious. Religious rituals and symbols of some kind have existed in every known human
society, and spiritual teachers of some kind are everywhere
accorded respect, and their wisdom is sought. Certainly,
organized religion has declined steeply in Europe over
the past century or more, and, although less marked, it
has also declined in America. But interest in religion generally is more lively than ever. Stamping out religion is no
more realistic than stamping out sex. And, just as we make
a moral distinction between good sexual relationships and
bad, so we must distinguish between good religion and

bad. In other words, having dismantled the theological edifices of the various religions, we must make pragmatic judgments about religious practices—in the same way that we make pragmatic judgments about political policies.

In order to make such judgments, we must first determine the essence of religion as a human phenomenon. In countries where Christianity, Islam, or Judaism has been predominant, it may seem that the common feature of all religion is belief in one or more supernatural beings. Yet Buddhism, Taoism, and some forms of Hinduism have no such belief, and Jainism is explicitly atheist. The gods of many tribal African and Amerindian religions are so human in character that their activities are often best understood as parables. A better definition is that religion is concerned with a person's inner being—one's emotions and attitudes—and religious rituals and symbols exist to exert some kind of influence on how we feel and think. Thus, while economic and political activity are directed toward changing our environment, religion is directed toward changing ourselves. Such a definition includes every religion. It also includes counseling and other forms of psychotherapy that have traditionally occurred within the orbit of religion, although they do not require any specific religious conviction or context.

With this broad definition it becomes quite simple to distinguish good and bad religion. Bad religion nurtures discontent, bigotry, and contempt, while good religion nurtures contentment, tolerance, and love. And this distinction is equally simple to apply. The religion motivating the terrorist hijackers on September 11 is manifestly bad; so are the forms of Catholicism and Protestantism that fuel hatred in Ireland; so are the forms of Judaism and

Islam that permit animosity between Israeli and Palestinian; and so is any religion, in any mosque, church, synagogue, or temple, that makes its adherents feel superior to others. As every great religious master has taught, spiritual pride and moral self-satisfaction are the parents of bigotry and contempt. Some religious doctrines, and some religious organizations promulgating doctrines, can be relatively innocuous. But the history of Christianity and Islam shows that dogmatic religion has an inherent tendency toward evil.

This tendency is rooted in the nature both of dogmas and of the organizations that dogmas spawn. By giving believers the impression that they already possess truth, dogmas convey to them that they have no need to change. Mere belief in the dogmas is sufficient. Thus, dogmas engender pride and self-satisfaction. The leaders of the organizations promoting these dogmas naturally judge their own success by the rate at which their organizations gain new adherents. So every religious organization tends to see other religious organizations as rivals that should be defeated and destroyed. And inevitably, they often use their rituals and symbols to whip up bigotry and contempt toward any creed but their own.

Within every religious tradition we can also find countless examples of goodness, not only within religious groups, but also reaching out beyond them. Jesus and Muhammad, both of whom showed kindness and generosity to anyone and everyone, are themselves shining examples. And among those within Christianity and Islam who are revered as saints, the most popular are those like Francis of Assisi who had no interest in rising up the religious hierarchy, but were aflame with love for all humanity. Indeed, one of the few pragmatic justifications for large-scale religious organizations is that they help to keep alive the memory of men and women whose goodness transcended all kinds of religious organization.

Despite the poor communication of past eras, religious insights managed to travel from one country to another, and from one continent to another. The interchange between Christianity and Islam from the very inception of Islam provides one example. Another example is the way in which Buddhism fused with the Confucian and Taoist traditions in China, renewing them both. And a little earlier, Zoroastrian ideas spread from eastern Iran to stimulate Greek and Roman religious ideas and to foster the spirit within Judaism that found its fullest expression in the teachings of Jesus and Paul—and later may have had a significant influence on Muhammad. While the globalization of creeds and sects has a long history of enmity, the globalization of religious wisdom has an equally long history of mutual enrichment. And the far better communication of the present era, which helps to discredit sectarian globalization, hugely enhances the opportunities for spiritual globalization.

Happily, these opportunities are being seized. People visit the buildings and enjoy the art of every religious tradition without discrimination. They read a spiritual article or book for the truths it might contain, regardless of the religious background of the author, and they attend courses on meditation and spirituality. The Buddha sitting in meditation has become as familiar an icon as Christ hanging from the cross. People are as happy to celebrate Arabic calligraphy as medieval stained glass. Far from being seen as an affront to the familiar church steeples, a minaret in a Western city is welcomed as a sign of spiritual diversity. The more spiritual wells there are from which they can drink, so people surmise, the better their inner thirst will be quenched.

In this modern pluralism, many people are thus quite naturally using religion as a means of inner transformation. The great Muslim philosophers such as al-Razi, Avicenna, and Averroes would rejoice at this. So also would many of the more prophetic Christian theologians of the past two hundred years. Friederich Schleiermacher, for example, pronounced in the early nineteenth century, "Religion is no kind of slavery, no kind of captivity; it is the place where you can be yourself—and the desire to be yourself is the beginning of faith." And he reinterpreted the entire body of religious doctrine in terms of psychological experience, showing how it can be a means of genuine personal fulfillment. In 1944 Dietrich Bonhoeffer, awaiting death in a Nazi prison, wrote of his contempt for "religious people who bring God onto the scene as the apparent solution to insoluble problems," and he advocated "religionless Christianity," which "simply means being a person—the person that God creates in us."

Religion after September 11

"What we saw on Tuesday," the Rev. Jerry Falwell, a leading Christian evangelist, opined on television a few days after September 11, "could be miniscule if in fact God continues to lift the curtain and allow the enemies of America

to give us probably what we deserve." His friend Pat
Robertson, another well-known evangelist, agreed. Jerry
Falwell continued, "I really believe that the pagans and the
abortionists and the feminists and the gays and lesbians
who are actively trying to make an alternative lifestyle . . .
all of them who have tried to secularize America, I point
the finger in their face and say, 'You helped this to happen.'" Falwell and Robertson were expressing a religious
attitude that in varying forms is familiar to Christian and
Muslim worshipers everywhere: God punishes those who
do not believe in him and ignore his will. Indeed, this view
is implicit in the very notion of religious dogma. The fear
of some kind of divine retribution, and the hope of divine
reward, is the ultimate reason why people adhere to religious dogmas for which there is no compelling evidence.

To the surprise of Falwell and Robertson, who are
accustomed to approval and adulation from conservative
Americans, there was widespread revulsion at Falwell's
remarks. Even President Bush distanced himself from
them, and this backlash may have contributed to Robertson's decision three months later to withdraw from political activity. In their attack on the World Trade Center, the
suicidal hijackers had exposed to America and the world
the cruel logic of dogmatic Islam. And Jerry Falwell had
shown that dogmatic Christianity follows a very similar
cruel logic. No one doubts that the logic itself, like that of
Ricardian economics, is impeccable, but its underlying
assumptions are not only highly dubious, like Ricardo's,
but also morally repugnant.

When people have replayed in their minds the television pictures of September 11, many have surely cried
out to themselves, "How can God allow this?" And some

have surely asked the corollary, "How can there be a God if things like this happen?" Thus they find themselves grappling with an issue that has nagged remorselessly at both Christianity and Islam ever since they began to define their beliefs: the problem of evil. At the center of their respective creeds both Christianity and Islam, in common with Judaism, assert the existence of a supreme being—God, Allah, Yahweh—who is omniscient and omnipotent, encompassing all knowledge and power. Yet the existence of evil—and there has never been a more vivid image of evil than airplanes being deliberately flown into the World Trade Center—suggests that God is morally neutral, with no preference for good over evil. The only other explanations are that God cannot foresee evil, and hence is not omniscient, or cannot prevent it, and hence is not omnipotent. But these explanations amount to a denial of the very existence of God. Both Christian and Muslim theologians have tried to surmount this problem by suggesting that God deliberately limits his power and knowledge in order to allow human beings some degree of freedom. But why, we are driven to ask, would God wish to limit his freedom if the consequences are so ghastly?

The apologists for organized Christianity and Islam have their reply, which has been repeated many times in the past: terrible evil and suffering has always existed, and yet their respective religions have survived. Indeed, in times of particular suffering, such as the Black Death in the fourteenth century, religion has thrived. But this complacency is misplaced. Suffering certainly pushes people toward religion, but they generally prefer more mystical forms of religion, which provide the inner means of coping with pain and distress. This was especially true in the fourteenth century when mystical Christianity reached its peak. And mysticism, by its nature, is heretical, since mystical experience has its own inner logic quite separate from the logic of dogma.

In the immediate aftermath of September 11 there was a significant rise in church attendance in America and other Western countries, as individuals and families sought spiritual solace, as well as answers to the religious questions that September 11 had raised. Within a few weeks, attendance fell back to its previous levels, as many realized that organized, dogmatic religion had nothing worthwhile to say. If the sermons and homilies broadcast in that period were typical of what was said in churches, most priests and ministers, while avoiding the grotesque insensitivity of Jerry Falwell, resorted to pious platitudes. But then something quite astonishing began to happen: many people became eager to learn about the other religions of the world, especially Islam. Sales of books on Islam and other religions rose rapidly, as did visits to religious centers of various kinds. To some extent, these people are curious to understand the religious beliefs that motivated the suicidal hijackers. But it seems that their interest goes much deeper than this. They sense that, although one kind of religion was the main cause of the horrors of September 11, a different kind of religion is also the only means of transcending those horrors. They want to reject dogmatism of all kinds, Christian as much as Islamic, and find forms of religion that are open and free.

A similar change may be occurring in Islamic countries. At first, even educated Muslims were ambivalent toward the attack on the World Trade Center. They were horrified by the carnage of innocent civilians, but also mesmerized by the audacity of the terrorists. As interviews at the time demonstrated, they wondered if the terrorists' success was a sign of divine blessing. Thus, the theology of Jerry Falwell, although unpopular in America, had widespread support within Islam. America's subsequent military victory in Afghanistan, however, undermined that theology, producing a profound change of mood among Muslims. It seems possible that if America and her allies are effective in the coming years in destroying the al Qaeda network throughout the world, many Muslims might turn decisively away from militancy, and from the dogmatism that underlies it. They too will seek forms of religion that are open and free. And this tendency will be hugely enhanced if the West starts to advocate global economic policies that enable Muslim countries to rise out of their poverty.

Toward Religious Freedom

Scattered across the countryside of rural India are innumerable temples and shrines. Worshipers visit these temples and shrines as and when they feel inclined, and they contribute money for their maintenance. Generally, a few priests, who perform ceremonies of various kinds, live nearby, and they go out from time to time to conduct weddings and funerals. The priests also farm some land or ply some craft, so they do not need to beg from worshipers. Some temples and shrines are entirely independent, and some belong to one of the many Hindu sects. But there is little rivalry between one temple and another, or between one sect and another, and many people enjoy visiting various types of temples.

In addition to the temples there are ashrams, where people go for spiritual teaching and advice. Ashrams come into being when a particular individual—a man or woman—gains a reputation for great wisdom. People are willing to travel a great distance to visit a teacher—a guru—whose style and insights appeal to them, and they build hostels near the teacher's house where they can stay. In many cases the ashram dies with the teacher, but sometimes one teacher appoints another as successor. A few teachers are mobile, wandering endlessly from place to place. The spiritual pupils of such a teacher may spend a few days or weeks each year wandering alongside him, or they may decide to wander permanently in the teacher's shadow.

In the far southwest of India there are also small churches, belonging to a Christian group that probably dates back to the third century. This group has come to be regarded almost as another Hindu sect; its members feel little inhibition about visiting Hindu temples, while many local Hindus are happy from time to time to worship in a church. There are a few Christian ashrams where Jesus Christ is presented as the guru. In some places Muslim mosques also fit harmoniously into this religious patchwork. Islam was originally brought to rural India by Sufis, who offered it simply as another spiritual path that someone might choose to follow. In the cities of North India under the Mughal empire, there was economic and political pressure on the people to convert to Islam, but in the remoter regions people became Muslim if they happened to be drawn to Sufi teaching.

Sadly, in certain parts of India in recent decades, Hinduism has acquired a militant face. Indeed, it was a militant Hindu who assassinated Gandhi, hating him for the respect and love he showed toward all religions. To some degree, Hinduism learned the spirit of militancy from the Christian missionaries who, from the sixteenth century on, were bent on tearing people from their religious and cultural roots and converting them to a quite different way of life. And to militant Christianity and Hinduism has now been added militant Islam. Many parts of the countryside, however, have so far been spared these poisons, and they continue to offer an example of how free, open religion may work.

The antiquity of this example is attested to in various texts, including the Buddhist scriptures. The Buddha was a wandering teacher in northern India with a substantial number of followers wandering with him. When he arrived at a town or village, he settled for a few days just outside, so that individuals living there were free to come and meet him. He never criticized the temples, and he treated their priests with courtesy. He also happily entered into conversation and debate with other spiritual teachers. Those who decided to acknowledge him as their guru, who remained in their homes, were expected also to remain loyal to their local temple. Justification for free, open religion is given in the *Bhagavad Gita,* an ancient Hindu text that commands almost universal respect: "There is no distinction between one religion and another. People may worship in any form they wish; the form of worship does not matter. What matters is the quality of love that religion nurtures."

Opinion polls seem to imply that this is the approach to religion that many in the West now favor. They have already broken the shackles of dogmatic religions and its organizations—or they probably never wore those shackles, since their parents or grandparents threw them off. Yet they feel the need for religion and want to satisfy that need without putting the shackles back on. The events of September 11 have both increased their dread of spiritual bonds and increased their hunger for spiritual food. At present this hunger is being satisfied by new teaching centers and by books and magazines. Some people are also feeding their souls by visits—pilgrimages—to churches and other sacred places. As yet, however, the conduct of worship, and the control of churches, remains almost entirely in the hands of doctrinal religious organizations. Our two greatest spiritual challenges are to find rituals and symbols that can uplift and transform individual worshipers, while requiring no formal belief on their part, and to hand over to popular control the places where rituals are traditionally enacted, and which are themselves powerful and benign symbols.

To a superficial observer, the Muslim world appears still to be chained fast to doctrinal religion, and the publicity gained by militant Islam gives the impression that the chains are tightening. Yet in Muslim countries where free votes are taken, militant political parties obtain minimal support. Western journalists and academics working in Muslim countries consistently report that most citizens have very moderate religious views, but that there is widespread antagonism to Western economic and political domination. The appeal of Islamic militancy, such as it is, lies not in its religious convictions, but in its offering a concrete means of expressing this antagonism. As and when political and economic equality is achieved, that appeal will evaporate. Meanwhile, the Muslim world is better placed than the West to find free and open forms of religion, because Sufism has remained far more vigorous than any of the Christian heresies.

When religions are free, they happily trade their symbols. Hindu sects are so open to new symbols that many temples and Hindu homes have pictures of Jesus and the Virgin Mary and hang star-shaped lanterns at Christmas. Thus, we can look forward to growing artistic enrichment in Western religion in the coming decades. But we may tentatively suggest a simple form that itself symbolizes free and open religion: the figure 0. This, of course, stands for zero, and in free and open religion, there are no beliefs. It also stands for the world, because the fruit of free and open religion is a sense of loving unity with all humanity and all that lives.

Conclusion: Freedom to Live in Peace

We may assume that the primary aim of the terrorists on September 11 was to spread terror. In this they succeeded beyond all measure. And as the outward signs of terror gradually fade with the passing weeks and months, it remains just below the surface, ready to erupt with even greater force as and when another terrorist attack is perpetrated.

This fear cannot ultimately be assuaged by protective measures or military action. Throughout the centuries, small gangs with deep political grievances, and usually with even deeper religious convictions, have always found ways of instilling fear in the general population, and modern weaponry and communications make this much easier. Yet fear can be transcended by hope. Despite the potential power of terrorism, it has usually not been exercised, and most societies at most times have lived in relative tranquility and security. This is because most societies at most times have found ways of addressing the potential terrorists' grievances and undermining their convictions in sufficient measure that terrorist gangs never form; or, if they do, the flow of recruits dries to a trickle, and supporters are no longer willing to shelter the remaining members. Since modern terrorism is a global phenomenon, our hope must lie in global society doing the same.

The central value of the West, which it shares with, and to some degree has inherited from, Islamic philosophy and law, is freedom — political and religious freedom. If we are to defeat terrorism, we must recognize that freedom is indivisible. Either everyone enjoys freedom, or ultimately no one can; either it is both political and religious, or it is neither. Thus we must strive for political and religious freedom across the entire world.

Political freedom means, in the first place, democracy and the rule of law; insofar as predominantly Muslim countries lack these things, they are betraying the *sharia*, which, properly understood, guarantees them. This must then provide the framework for genuine economic freedom: not the false freedom that allows global corporations to turn poorer countries into virtual economic colonies, but the freedom that enables individuals to create businesses that meet their compatriots' needs and thence grow and employ others.

Religious freedom means, in the first place, mutual tolerance and protection for all faiths under the law; insofar as predominantly Muslim countries lack these things, they are also betraying the *sharia*, which, properly understood, guarantees them. This must then provide the framework for genuine spiritual freedom: not the false freedom in which global sects strive for control over people's minds, but the freedom that enables individuals to find insight and inspiration from any and every source as it suits them.

The fruit of political and religious freedom is peace — at two levels. First, there is peace between peoples. When people enjoy both the prosperity that political freedom brings, and the contentment that religious freedom brings, mutual hostility becomes unthinkable. Secondly, there is peace between humanity and the planet itself. When people have control over their own economic welfare, they look after the environment on which it depends, and when they have control over their own spirits, they are happy with whatever their environment yields.

Fear of terrorism is horribly and painfully passive. There is almost nothing that most of us can do to protect ourselves. But the hope of freedom and peace can be active; every individual, family, and neighborhood can contribute. We can begin to reduce our consumption of goods, especially primary products such as exotic fruits and flowers, from far-off lands. If we work in large corporations, we can try to persuade them to disengage from activities in poorer countries. We can contribute to nonprofit organizations that offer education in the West to students from poorer countries, and we can welcome such people into our homes. We can educate ourselves in the cultures and traditions of other countries and continents. We can withdraw from any involvement in doctrinal religious organizations and participate in groups that practice religious openness. We can learn to be contented with what we already have — and then learn to be contented with a little less. And, of course, we can exercise our democratic rights in the direction of freedom. Thus we can all become foot soldiers in the *jihad* for peace.

A military and financial *jihad* against global terrorism, as America and her allies are waging, will take a very long time, as American leaders have warned. And although it will constrain terrorist activity, ultimately, as many Western experts admit, it cannot achieve any final victory. A *jihad* for peace, waged by striving for political and religious freedom across the world, will take an equally long time. But, happily, it can be won—and victory will render the first *jihad* unnecessary.

Appendix 1

Muhammad, Islam, Judaism, and Christianity

The Prophet Muhammad

Muhammad was born around 570 C.E. in Mecca, the major city of the Arabian peninsula. Arabian society at the time consisted of a series of tribes, most of which were nomadic. Muhammad belonged to the dominant tribe, the Quraysh, which specialized in commerce. His father, a merchant, died before he was born, and his mother died when he was aged only six. He was raised by his uncle, also a merchant, and by his grandfather, a man renowned for his saintliness.

In the center of Mecca was a large sacred enclosure — the Grand Mosque — at the center of which was a cube-shaped temple, the Ka'aba. Arabs from all over the peninsula came to the Ka'aba on an annual pilgrimage. Some Arabs, such as Muhammad's grandfather, were devoutly monotheistic, believing in one God, whom they called Allah. They believed that Abraham, the founder of Judaism, and his son Ishmael built the Ka'aba, on the site of the first dwelling built by Adam, the first human being. But most Arabs believed in a variety of divine beings; and the Ka'aba was filled with sacred statues depicting these beings. Muhammad from an early age adopted his grandfather's monotheism.

When he had grown up, Muhammad worked first as a shepherd. Then a wealthy widow, Khadijah, employed him as a merchant, making him the leader of a caravan

taking goods to Jerusalem. This trip brought him into
direct contact with a wide variety of Christians and Jews
and had a profound spiritual impression on him. When
he returned to Mecca, Khadijah offered herself to him in
marriage, and although he was aged only twenty-five, and
she was in her forties, he accepted her. They lived happily
together and had six children.

His marriage gave Muhammad the financial security
to devote more time to prayer and meditation. He regularly went off alone, often for several days and nights at
a time, to the mountains near Mecca to be close to God. On
one occasion, in the year 610, a spiritual presence, whom he
identified as the angel Gabriel, showed him some words
and ordered him to recite them. Gabriel then ordered him
to memorize the words and recite them to others. These
were the first phrases of the book that became known as
the Koran, which means "recitation." A gap of two years
ensued before the next revelations, and then they continued regularly for a further twenty-two years.

At first, Muhammad spoke about his revelations only
to individuals who might be interested; his wife Khadijah
and his nephew Ali were the first to believe in their authen-
ticity. Then he received divine instruction to preach publicly. Many ordinary men and women were impressed,
and became Muslim, "one who surrenders to God." However, the Quraysh religious leaders feared that Muhammad's ideas threatened their own position. They made various attempts to murder him, and they tried to destroy the
livelihoods of Muslims. At one stage, a large group of
Muslims fled to Ethiopia, where the Christian ruler protected them.

To the north of Mecca lay the smaller city of Medina,
with a population consisting of two Arab tribes, who
were perpetually in conflict, and a community of Jews.

In 622 the tribal elders joined together in inviting Muhammad to be their leader and judge. So Muhammad instructed all Muslims in Mecca to escape to Medina under cover of night, and he followed them. This emigration—known as *hijrah*—is regarded as the inception of Islam as a distinct religion. Muhammad drew up a charter for Medina that conferred on everyone the right to live freely, maintaining their customs and practicing their religion, without fear of persecution or ill-favor. Their only common obligation was to support one another against any enemy. The charter was accepted, and for the first time in many years Medina was at peace.

A large portion of the Medina population converted to Islam, and with their support, Muhammad decided to mount a war against his own tribe. He also used the charter to persuade many non-Muslims to join him, arguing that the Quraysh elders were his enemies. He began by attacking caravans from Mecca, thus undermining the Quraysh economy. The Quraysh then sent a large army against him, which he defeated. After the Quraysh formed a new army to besiege Medina, Muhammad overcame it through a remarkable act of deception, tricking the Quraysh leader into believing that his forces were hopelessly divided. After several more battles and skirmishes, Muhammad led his troops to Mecca itself. His reputation had risen so high that all resistance melted away, and he entered the city without bloodshed.

Muhammad rode straight to the Ka'aba, where he destroyed almost all the sacred images—preserving only a picture of Jesus and Mary. He proved gentler with his former enemies, pardoning all the Quraysh leaders on condition that they swore their fealty to him. He now turned his attention to the other Arab tribes. Although some were incensed by his desecration—as they saw it—

of the Ka'aba, they could offer no match for his army, which was by far the largest ever assembled in Arabia. Within a short time, almost the entire peninsula was under Muhammad's control, and tribe after tribe concluded that Allah was more powerful than their ancestral deities.

Khadijah had died in 619, before the migration to Medina. Although polygamy was widely practiced in Arabia, Muhammad had lived monogamously with her. However, in the years after her death he acquired twelve wives. Most of them were mature widows with whom he had no sexual relations. By committing himself to care for them, he was fulfilling the main social purpose of polygamy. Among these wives, two were Jewish, and one was Christian. He expected his wives to share his way of life, which was extremely austere. He ate little, and his meals were simple; he lived in mud huts; he slept on the floor; and he wore old clothes, sewing patches on them as need arose. He regarded all goods as loans from God, and so, whenever he was given something beyond his immediate needs, he passed it on to the poor. And he was humble, demanding no special treatment and happily sharing domestic chores with his wives and menial tasks with his followers.

Muhammad's victory over Mecca occurred in 629. But he fell ill soon afterward. While his rule was spreading across Arabia, his own body was steadily weakening. He died in Medina in 632, aged sixty-three.

The Koran and the Hadith

The essence of Islam is that there is a single supreme being, Allah, that Muhammad is a prophet of Allah, and that the Koran is the prophecies given to Muhammad by Allah.

The Koran consists of 114 chapters *(sura)*, which are arranged in order of length, the longer preceding the shorter. The whole book is about four-fifths the size of the New Testament. Sometimes Allah speaks directly in the first person, but more often Allah is referred to—or refers to himself—in the third person.

The theology of the Koran is quite simple: Allah created the universe and is the supreme force within it. Human beings are Allah's highest creation, and he gives them each a soul as well as a body. He makes his will known in every age and to every nation through prophets, among whom are included Jesus and the Hebrew prophets. And he requires human beings to obey his will. Allah has also created angels, who guide and strengthen people in obeying his will, and devils, who tempt them to be disobedient. Everyone has two guardian angels whose main role is to record every deed. Eventually, there will be a day of judgment, when the records of the dead and living alike will be examined; the good will be taken to everlasting paradise, while the wicked will be cast down into hell. However, Allah is a merciful and compassionate judge, so he will be lenient in assessing evil deeds.

There are five main laws of Islam *(sharia)*, derived from the Koran, that define Muslim practice. These are known as the five pillars of Islam. The first is profession of faith *(shahadah)*. This refers to the Islamic creed: "There is no god but God, and Muhammad is his true messenger." To become a Muslim, a person must say these words, and sincerely believe them, in front of two witnesses.

The second pillar is worship *(salat)*. Muslims may offer prayers of petition and pleading *(du'ah)* at any time and in any place. But they have a specific obligation to engage in worship five times a day—at dawn, at noon, in the afternoon, at sunset, and at night. Beforehand, they should wash. Then they must stand on clear ground and face Mecca. The words and the movements are prescribed and must be followed precisely. If possible, individuals should worship in the company of others; if for some compelling reason a particular act of worship is missed, it should be performed later. Almost every mosque—the Muslim place of worship—has a tower or minaret. From the top of the minaret a voice cries out the profession of faith at the times of worship, reminding people of their duty. In addition to this daily routine, all adult male Muslims are required to gather in their local mosque for congregational prayers each Friday. Each congregation appoints a minister *(imam)* to lead Friday prayers, and he may also preach.

The third pillar is almsgiving *(zakat)*. Muslim households are required to set aside part of their annual income for the poor and sick. This should comprise the surplus after the needs of children and relatives have been met. Although many congregations have funds into which contributions can be made, individuals are free to choose how best to help those in need. However, they should avoid making any show of their charity.

The fourth pillar is fasting *(saum)*. For a month each year—the month of Ramadan, when Muhammad received the first revelations—Muslims do not eat, drink, or have sex during daylight hours. The Islamic calendar consists of twelve lunar months, so Ramadan falls slightly earlier each year. The purpose of fasting is partly to cultivate inner peace and partly to identify with those suffering famine and drought. As a communal practice, it greatly strengthens Muslim solidarity. The very old and young, invalids, and expectant and nursing mothers are excused from fasting, and soldiers on campaigns and travelers on long journeys are allowed to postpone it. At the end of Ramadan is the festival of Eid, when gifts are exchanged and a great meal is eaten.

The fifth pillar is pilgrimage *(hajj)*. All Muslims able to afford it are expected to make a pilgrimage to the Ka'aba once in their lifetime. The main time of pilgrimage is two months after Ramadan. Nowadays, about two million people each year converge on Mecca. Those wishing to make additional pilgrimages are encouraged to go at another time of the year.

After the death of Muhammad his sayings *(hadith)* on a wide variety of subjects were written down, and various collections began to circulate. From a combination of these sayings and the teachings of the Koran, various other Muslim practices emerged. The most notable concern marriage, the position of women, and diet. Islam encourages monogamy, but allows a man to have up to four wives, so long as he can afford to keep them. Husband and wife are required to treat one another with respect and have an obligation to satisfy one another's sexual needs. Divorce is regarded as evil and is only permissible if a marriage has become intolerable. The husband makes the decision. Women are allowed to inherit property, a notable advance on pre-Islamic Arab practice which treated women themselves as property. Nowhere is the veiling or seclusion of women stipulated, but women are told to behave and dress with modesty. The dietary rules *(halal)* are similar to those of Judaism: pork and blood products are forbidden; and the slaughter of animals is by cutting the throat and letting the blood drain away. Alcohol is forbidden.

Relationship with Judaism and Christianity

When the Jews were forced to flee from Jerusalem in 70 C.E. after the Romans suppressed their revolt, some undoubtedly came to Arabia. It is probable that they converted a substantial number of local people to their faith, and then intermarried. Thus, in Muhammad's time, there was a substantial Jewish population in Medina and other towns and settlements in the northern part of the Arabian peninsula. It may have been through their influence that many other Arabs, such as Muhammad's grandfather, adopted monotheism. And it came to be believed by monotheistic Arabs, Jews and non-Jews alike, that the entire Arab race was descended from Ishmael, and thence Abraham. The Bible records how, with the permission of his wife Sarah, Abraham had sex with Hagar, his wife's slave. But when Hagar became pregnant, she was contemptuous of Sarah, who had never conceived, and Sarah in turn treated her cruelly. The biblical story ends with Hagar fleeing. Islamic tradition takes up the tale, relating that, after Hagar had given birth to Ishmael, Abraham took them to Mecca, then barren and unpopulated, and abandoned them. By a miracle, a spring appeared, which provided water for them. Soon afterward, a group of Bedouin asked to settle there in order to take advantage of the water, and Hagar granted permission on condition that the land should remain the property of Ishmael and his descendants. Ishmael grew up and married an Arab girl. Then Abraham returned and, with Ishmael's help, built the Ka'aba, the first shrine to the one true God.

Abraham figures prominently in the Koran, and Islam is presented as a reaffirmation of the faith that God revealed through Abraham many centuries earlier. Thus, Muhammad saw no distinction between Islam and Judaism. However, if he expected the Jews in Medina to acknowledge him as a prophet, he was disappointed. While they seem initially to have welcomed him as a peacemaker, few accepted Islam or supported him in his war against the Quraysh in Mecca. Indeed, some Jews elsewhere, most notably in the northern town of Khaibar, actively sided with the Quraysh. Shortly before marching on Mecca, Muhammad attacked and defeated the Khaibar Jews; other Jewish communities in the region submitted without a fight. Muhammad allowed the Jews freedom to practice their religion and merely imposed a poll tax on them. This became the model that the caliphs followed in the treatment of both Jews and Christians throughout the Arab empire.

In addition to the Jewish Arabs, there were scattered communities of Christians in Arabia in Muhammad's time. Indeed, the Koran refers to an invasion of the Mecca and Medina region by a Christian army from southern Arabia, an event that occurred in 570 C.E. And the willingness of the original Muslims of Mecca to seek refuge under Ethiopia's Christian king suggests that they saw in Christianity a religion similar to their own. But the Koran rejects some important aspects of the Christian story as told in the New Testament, and it even more emphatically rejects the central dogmas of Christianity as they had evolved in the centuries prior to Muhammad. According to the Koran, Jesus was not crucified, but was taken directly up to heaven by God. The story of the crucifixion, which it regards as a slander, emerged because another person resembling Jesus was killed in his place. Therefore, Islam denies the Christian dogma of redemption, by which the death of Christ was a sacrifice for human sin. Islam also denies the dogma of Christ's divinity, seeing Christ only as a prophet, like Muhammad himself. Thus, the worship of Christ is to Muslims idolatrous. Nonetheless, the Koran expresses great reverence for Mary, the mother of Jesus, and affirms the virgin birth. By preserving a picture of Jesus and Mary in the Ka'aba, Muhammad demonstrated his own respect.

Some Key Dates

381. Council of Constantinople when the Christian (Nicene) creed was agreed upon.

451. Council of Chalcedon, which agreed that Christ had a divine and a human nature.

570. Probable date of Muhammad's birth.

610. The first words of the Koran were received.

622. Emigration of Muslims from Mecca to Medina *(hijra)*.

624. Battle of Badr, Muhammad's first major military victory.

629. Muhammad's triumphal entry into Mecca.

632. Muhammad's death.

639. Muslim conquest of Egypt.

661. Capital of Muslim empire established in Damascus.

732. Muslims defeated at Poitiers, France.

750. Capital of Muslim empire established in Baghdad.

785. Construction begins on Great Mosque in Cordova, Spain.

1054. Separation of Roman Catholic and Eastern Orthodox churches.

1099. Capture of Jerusalem by the Crusaders.

1187. Saladin's recapture of Jerusalem.

1453. Fall of Constantinople to the Ottoman Turks.

1492. End of Muslim rule in Spain.

1683. Failure of Ottoman siege of Vienna.

1801. First major Islamic terrorist act, which occurred in Arabia.

1858. End of Mughal rule in India, and formal establishment of British rule.

1896. Foundation of the Zionist movement.

1922. The last Ottoman sultan deposed.

1928. Muslim Brotherhood founded.

1947. Pakistan established as an Islamic state.

1948. The foundation of the state of Israel.

1979. Islamic revolutionary regime established in Iran.

1981. Egyptian Islamic Jihad's assassination of Egyptian President Anwar Sadat.

1993. First Islamic terrorist attack on the World Trade Center, New York.

1996. Capture of Kabul by the Taliban.

1997. Killing by Islamic terrorists of seventy tourists in Luxor, Egypt.

2001. Destruction of the World Trade Center by Islamic terrorists.

2001. Fall of Taliban regime in Afghanistan.

Appendix 2

A Guide to Further Reading

There are many introductions to Islam. One of the best is *Islam: The Straight Path* by John L. Esposito (Oxford University Press, 1988). Esposito looks at the origins and message of Islam, its religious practices, its history, and the modern Islamic scene. Another good introduction is *Islam* by Ruqaiyyah Maqsood (NTC/Contemporary Publishing, 1997). Maqsood, having described the life of Muhammad and the teachings of the Koran, gives considerable detail about Islamic worship and the Muslim way of life. Although first published almost half a century ago, *Islam*, by Alfred Guillaume (Penguin Books, 1990), remains very valuable; it is especially good on Islamic philosophy and mysticism.

A highly readable biography of Muhammad is available: *Muhammad: A Biography of a Prophet* by Karen Armstrong (HarperCollins, 1992). Like every story of Muhammad's life, it is heavily based on the records compiled about a century after his death by Ibn Ishaq. This compilation was translated by A. Guillaume as *The Life of Muhammad* (Oxford University Press, 1955). It should be said that scholars are now beginning to question the accuracy of Ibn Ishaq's work, with some even suggesting that we have almost no certain knowledge about Muhammad's life.

The two main university presses in England have each produced general surveys, both of which are highly readable and well illustrated. *The Oxford History of Islam*, edited by John L. Esposito (Oxford University Press, 1999), contains valuable chapters of the various aspects of Islamic culture. The *Cambridge Encyclopedia of the Middle East and North Africa*, edited by Trevor Mostyn and Albert Hourani (Cambridge University Press, 1988), has a greater emphasis on the social and economic life of the various countries of the region.

An excellent history of the relationship between Islam and the rest of the world is *Islam and the World* by Malise Ruthven (Penguin Books, 2000). The current edition takes the story to 1999. The focus of the book is political and demonstrates with admirable clarity the complex interaction of religion and politics. A highly informative book on the roots of Islamic militancy is *Radical Islam* by Emmanuel Sivan (Yale University Press, 1990). There are, of course, many Muslims in the United States. Their life and background is explored in *Islam in America* by Jane Smith (Columbia University Press, 1999).

Books on Sufism, the mystical and heretical form of Islam, used to be rare, but recently have become more numerous. *Mystical Islam* by Julian Baldick (New York University Press, 1989) is very clear and accurate. A somewhat deeper book is *Sufism* by Carl W. Ernst (Shambhala, 1997).

I also commend my own collection of readings from original Muslim sources, *366 Readings from Islam* (The Pilgrim Press, 2000). This contains extracts from the Koran and Ibn Ishaq's *Life,* as well as selections from the works of Sufi mystics and Islamic philosophers.

Index

Abelard, 86
Abraham, 116
Afghanistan, 16, 21–22, 78
Africa, European colonization in, 15, 57
African National Congress (ANC), 78
agriculture, 66
al-Afghani, 19–20
al-Aqsa, 9–10
al-Banna, Hasan, 20
alcohol, Islam and, 115
Alexandria, Egypt, 35–36
Alexius Comnenus, Byzantine emperor, 9
algebra, 43
Algeria, 22
al-Ghazali, 38–39, 41
al-Haytham, 43
al-Khwarizmi, 43
almsgiving, 114
al Qaeda, 23
al-Razi, 37, 44
al-Shafii, 46
al-Wahhab, 19, 22–23
ANC. See African National Congress
angels, 113

anti-Semitism, and Zionism, 24, 26–27
Arab empire, 7–8, 12–13, 35–36
Arabia, 16
Arabic language, 36, 40
Arabic numerals, 43
Arabs, Palestinian, 28, 30
Arianism, 34–35, 86, 89–90
Aristotle, 35–36, 39–40
ashrams, 100
Asia: economies of, 63, 69; European colonization in, 15, 57
astronomy, 42–43
Augustine of Hippo, 50, 85
Austria, 26
autocratic governments, and war on terrorism, 78–79
automobiles, controls on, 74–75
Averroes, 39–40
Avicenna, 37–38, 40, 44
awareness of Western affluence, 64–65

Bacon, Francis, 39
Baghdad, 11, 36

Balfour Declaration, 27

Begin, Menachem, 21

Bernard of Clairvaux, 39

Bhagavad Gita, 101–2

Black Death, 97–98

Blair, Tony, 30

Bonhoeffer, Dietrich, 95

Boxer rebellion, 2

Britain: and colonization, 14–16, 61; and free trade, 56–57; and Islam, 2; legacy of, 68; and Zionism, 25–28

Buddhism, 94, 101

bureaucracy, and Ottoman empire, 12, 14

Bush, George W., 30, 51, 96

Byzantine empire, 9

caliphs, 11, 45

Camp David Accords, 21

capitalism: and colonialism, 15; development of, 14; momentum of, 19–20; resistance to, 2, 72; Ricardo on, 55–60; versus simplicity, 74

Catholicism, 86–87

China, 2, 52–53, 66, 94

Christianity: exclusivity of, 83–84; false assumptions about, 85–90; globalization and, 81–84; in India, 100–101; and inquiry, 13, 36; and Islam, 33–36, 115–17; Muhammad and, 8, 33, 112, 117; and roots of Islam, 33–35; schism in,

10; on warfare, 50–51; and Zionism, 25–26. *See also* West

Churchill, Winston, 71

Clement, 35

colonialism, 13–18; legacy of, 18, 29–31, 68

commerce: Europe and, 17–18; globalization and, 55–60

comparative advantage: and migration, 67; theory of, 56

conflict: between Islam and West, 1–3, 7–31; Israeli-Palestinian, 79–80

Confucius, 94

consensus, 77; and law, 47

Constantinople, 9, 12

cooperation between Islam and West, 3–4, 33–53

creeds, globalization of, 81–85

Crusades, 2, 8–11

Dante Alighieri, 8

demand, Ricardo on, 58

democracy, 77; Islam and, 45; in Middle East, 80; Rousseau on, 76

devils, 113

diet, Islam and, 115

Disraeli, Benjamin, 24

Dome of the Rock, 9–10

Donatists, 85–86

du'ah, 113

Dutch, 14

East India Company, 15
economic envy, 29, 64–65
economic freedom, 106
economic theory, Ricardian,
    55–60
Egypt, 16, 22; Alexandria,
    35–36
Egyptian Islamic Jihad
    (EIJ), 21
Eid, 114
environmental pollution, 73
Ethiopia, 35, 110, 117
Europe. *See* West
European Union, and tariffs,
    69–70
evangelical Christianity, 31;
    and Zionism, 25–26
evil: Avicenna on, 37–38; and
    September 11, 96–97
exclusivity of Christianity,
    83–84
expertise, globalization of,
    65–70

Falwell, Jerry, 95–96
Farisi, 44
fasting, 114
fear, of terrorism, 105, 107
France, 15–16, 76
Francis of Assisi, 93
freedom: God and, 97–98;
    individual versus collective,
    75–76; to live in peace,
    105–8; political, 75–80;
    religious, 99–103; types of,
    4–5, 106–7

free trade: in India, 61;
    theory of, 55–60
Friedman, Milton, 55
fundamentalism, 6, 41, 48,
    92–93, 95–96

Gabriel, 110
Gama, Vasco da, 14
Gandhi, 2, 60–61, 101
Geber, 52
General Agreement on Tariffs
    and Trade (GATT), 60
general will, 76–77
Germany, 16, 73; and
    Zionism, 24–26
Giuliani, Rudy, 71
globalization: of civilization,
    53; and freedom, 79; of
    goods and capital, 55–60;
    intellectual, 4; of people
    and expertise, 65–70; and
    religion, 81–85; resistance
    to, 2, 61, 69; spiritual,
    90–95
Gnosticism, 34–35
Grand Mosque, 109
Greek religion, 94
gurus, 100

hadith, 115
hajj, 115
halal, 115
Hallaj, 87
harmony between Islam and
    West, 3–4, 33–53
Hasan al-Basr, 87

hatred: causes of, 1–3, 7–31; well of, 2

heresy, 34–35, 85–86; mysticism and, 97–98; versus orthodoxy, 88–90

Herman the German, 40

Herzl, Theodor, 26–28, 80

Hess, Moses, 25

hijrah, 111

Hinduism, 37, 99–102

Hippocrates, 44

Holocaust, and Zionism, 28

hope, 105–8

human nature, and religion, 91

Hunayn, 42

Hussein, Saddam, 88

Ibn al-Shatir, 43

Ibn Ishaq, 33, 49

Ibn Majid, 14

Ibn Rushd. *See* Averroes

Ibn Sina. *See* Avicenna

imam, 114

IMF. *See* International Monetary Fund

immigration, 72; laws on, recommendations for, 65–70

imperialism, Western, 13–18

India: British and, 2, 57; economic status of, 60–62; independence movement in, 2; Islam and, 12, 52; religious flexibility in, 99–102; Western imperialism and, 15

intellectual globalization, 4

International Monetary Fund (IMF), 56, 60, 75

investment: in United States, 58; Western, issues with, 63–64

Iran, 36, 88; empire of, 12; revolution in, 21–22

Iraq, 16

Isfahan, 12

Ishmael, 116

Islam: after September 11, 98–99; Christianity and Judaism and, 33–36, 115–17; false assumptions about, 85–90; free and open version of, 102–3; globalization and, 84–85; in India, 100–101; invasion of Europe, 2, 7; law and politics in, 45–48; militant, 3, 19–23, 103; philosophy and theology in, 35–41, 112–15; pillars of, 113–14; and political freedom, 76–77; roots of, Christianity and, 33–35; and science, 20, 41–44; and warfare, 48–51

Islamic civilization, 33–53; legacy of, 52–53

Islam-Western relations: conflict, 1–3, 7–31; incompatibility in, 19–20; love and respect, 3–4, 33–53

"Is mutual love and respect possible?", 3–4, 33–53

Israel, 30–31; founding of, 23–28

Israeli-Palestinian conflict, 79–80
Italy, 16

Japan, 69, 73–74
Jerusalem, Muhammad and, 8–9
Jesus, 81–84, 93, 111, 117; modern views of, 90
jihad: for peace, 107–8; spiritual, 49
Jordan, 16
Judaism: and Islam, 36, 115–17; Muhammad and, 9, 112; and Zionism, 23–28, 30–31
judges, 77, 111
just war theory, 50

Ka'aba, 109, 111–12, 116
Keynes, John Maynard, 55, 59
Khadijah, 8, 109–10, 112
Khomeini, Ayatollah, 21–22
Koran, 112–15; on Abraham, 116; and Christianity, 34–35; and law, 46; writing of, 7, 110

labor: in Asia, 63–64; difficulties of, 62–63; Ricardian economics and, 56, 59–60
law: evolution of, 47–48; Muslims and, 13, 45–48; roots of, 46–47. *See also* *sharia*

Lebanon, 16
Logos, 82–83
Luther, Martin, 41

Mahdi, 88
Malaysia, 63
Mandela, Nelson, 78
marriage, Islam and, 112, 115
Marx, Karl, 24
Mary, 111, 117
material simplicity, 74
mathematics, Muslims and, 41–44
Mecca, 109–10
medicine, Muslims and, 41–44
Medina, 110–11, 116
Michael the Scot, 40
migration of peoples, 65–70
militant Hinduism, 101
militant Islam, 3, 103; development of, 19–23
Mongols, 11
Muhammad, 81–84, 93, 109–12; assassination attempts on, 35, 49; and Christianity, 8, 33, 112, 117; and Jerusalem, 8–9; and Judaism, 9, 23–24, 112; and political freedom, 76–77; and politics, 45; revelations of, 7; sayings of, 115; and warfare, 48–49, 110–12
Muhammad ibn Saud, 19
mujahideen, 78

Muslim, definition of, 110
Muslim Brotherhood, 20–21
mysticism, and heresy, 97–98

organized religion, 89–90, 93–94, 102
Origen, 35
orthodoxy, triumph of, 88–90
Osama bin Laden, 23, 78
Ottoman empire, 11–13; and science, 41–42

Pakistan, 68
Palestine: Arabs in, 28, 30; British and, 16, 25–28
Paris, university of, 40
Paul of Tarsus, 82
peace, 105–8; in Europe, 14; Judaism and, 25; politics of, 55–80; Ramadan and, 114; religion of, 4–6, 81–103
Pelagianism, 86, 89–90
people, globalization of, 65–70
Persia, 16. *See also* Iran
Petty, William, 69
Philo, 82
philosophy: in Europe, 39–40; Islam and, 35–41
pilgrimage, 115
Plato, 35–36, 40
pluralism, in religion, 94–95
political freedom, 75–80, 106
politics: after September 11, 70–75; Muslims and, 45–48; of peace, 55–80; of Zionism, 26–27
polygamy, 112
prayer, Avicenna on, 38
printing, 52–53
profession of faith, 113
progress: Muslims and, 13; Western, 18
Protestants, 41, 86–87

questions, 1–6; "Is mutual love and respect possible?", 3–4, 33–53; "What can we do — politically?", 4–6, 55–80; "What can we do — religiously?", 4–6, 81–103; "Why do they hate us?", 1–3, 7–31
Qutb, Sayyid, 20

Rabia, 87
Ramadan, 114
religion: after September 11, 5, 91, 95–99; essence of, 92; European view of, in nineteenth century, 17; false assumptions about, 85–90; good versus bad, 5–6, 91–94; of peace, 4–6, 81–103
religious freedom, 99–103, 106–7
Renaissance, European, 4, 40–41
resistance: to globalization, 61, 69; to Western influence, 2–3

respect between Islam and West, 3–4, 33–53

Ricardian economic theory, 55–60; critique of, 60–65, 75

Ricardo, David, 55

rituals: nature of, 92; open, 102

Robertson, Pat, 96

Romanus IV, emperor of Constantinople, 9

Rome, 52; religion of, 94

Roosevelt, Franklin Delano, 59

Roosevelt, Theodore, 57

Rothschild, Edmond de, 26

Rousseau, Jean-Jacques, 75–76

Sadat, Anwar, 21

Salah al-din, 10–11

salat, 113–14

saum, 114

Say, Jean-Baptiste, 58

Schleiermacher, Friederich, 95

science, 2; Islam and, 20; Muslims and, 13, 39, 41–44

sects, globalization of, 81–85

Seljuk dynasty, 9

September 11, 2001: politics after, 70–75; questions following, 1–6; religion after, 5, 91, 95–99

Shaftesbury, earl of, 25

shahadah, 113

sharia, 46, 113; evolution of, 47–48; Qutb and, 21; Taliban and, 22; and terrorism, 51; on warfare, 49

Shia Muslims, 88

Shiites, 11

South Africa, 78

South Korea, 63

Spain, reconquest of, 8

spiritual globalization, 90–95

suffering: Ramadan and, 114; religion and, 97–98

Sufism, 87–89, 100–101

sultans, 11

sunna, 46–47

Sunni Muslims, 88

supply, Ricardo on, 58

Switzerland, 76

symbols: globalization of, 90–95; nature of, 92

Syria, 16

Taliban, 21–22; and *sharia*, 48; and Shia Muslims, 88

Taoism, 94

tariffs, 56–57, 59–60; protective, 69

teachers, law on, 48

Tel Aviv, 27

terrorism: fear of, 105, 107; *sharia* and, 51; Zionism and, 28

Thailand, 63

theology, Islam and, 35–41, 113

Thirty Years' War, 14, 86
Thomas Aquinas, 39–40, 50
trade unions, 60
Turkey, 16

United Nations, 28
United States: economic
　development of, 57–58; and
　Islam, 30; and Zionism, 26
University of Paris, 40
Urban II, pope, 10

Victoria, queen of Great
　Britain, 15
Vienna, 12

Wahabbiot tradition, 22
Wailing Wall, 9
Waldes, preacher, 10–11
Wali Allah, Shah, 19
warfare: conditions for, 49;
　Islam and, 48–51;
　Muhammad and, 48–49,
　110–12; religious, 85–90
war on terrorism, 71–72;
　autocratic governments
　and, 78–79
West: economic development
　of, 55–60; and freedom,

106; imperialism of, 13–18;
　and Judaism, 24–25;
　relations with Islam (*See*
　Islam-Western relations);
　and September 11, 2001,
　1–3
"What can we do—
　politically?", 4–6, 55–80
"What can we do—
　religiously?", 4–6, 81–103
"Why do they hate us?", 1–3,
　7–31
wisdom: globalization of,
　90–95; personification of,
　82–83
women, Islam and, 115
Word, 82–83
World Trade Organization
　(WTO), 56, 60, 70
worship, 113–14
WTO. *See* World Trade
　Organization

Yemen, 16

zakat, 114
zero, 43, 103
Zionism, 23–28, 30
Zoroastrianism, 94

The Author

Robert Van de Weyer worked for twenty years as a university lecturer in political economy and is minister of a church dedicated to the unity of all religions. He is the author and editor of more than fifty books in the fields of politics, economics, religion, and history—subjects brought together in this wide-ranging work.